D1756398

THROUGH A MAZE BLINDFOLD

GW 3483020 0

THROUGH
A MAZE
BLINDFOLD

My experience of
Interstitial Cystitis

Janet Baird

The Book Guild Ltd

First published in Great Britain in 2016 by
The Book Guild Ltd
9 Priory Business Park
Wistow Road, Kibworth
Leicestershire, LE8 0RX
Freephone: 0800 999 2982
www.bookguild.co.uk
Email: info@bookguild.co.uk
Twitter: @bookguild

Copyright © 2016 Janet Baird

The right of Janet Baird to be identified as the author of this
work has been asserted by her in accordance with the
Copyright, Design and Patents Act 1988.

All rights reserved. No part of this publication may be
reproduced, transmitted, or stored in a retrieval system, in any form or
by any means, without permission in writing from the publisher,
nor be otherwise circulated in any form of binding or cover other
than that in which it is published and without a similar
condition being imposed on the subsequent purchaser.

Typeset in Garamond

Printed and bound in the UK by
TJ International, Padstow, Cornwall

ISBN 978 1 910 87840 8

British Library Cataloguing in Publication Data.
A catalogue record for this book is available from the British Library.

MIX
Paper from
responsible sources
FSC® C013056
www.fsc.org

In memory of Brenda

DISCLAIMER

Janet Baird is qualified in Nutritional Medicine, Iridology and is also a registered Bach Flower Practitioner. She does not have any orthodox medical qualifications.

Everything the author has written in this book is based on experience and private research. The content of this book is not intended to be a substitute for professional medical advice, diagnosis, or treatment. Always seek the advice of a physician or other qualified health provider with any questions you may have regarding a medical condition.

Removal of mercury fillings MUST be done by a qualified mercury free dentist who knows the dangers and uses the correct protocol to protect the patient.

Contents

Prologue

The Divine Weaver

Mans life is laid in the loom of time
To a pattern he does not see
While the weaver works and the shuttles fly
To the end of eternity

Not till the loom is silent
And shuttles cease to fly.
Does God reveal the pattern
Explain the reason why.

Our destinies are NOT a continual line, but are like a maze with many branching paths. If an earlier action had been different then a future event would have been different. Once a fork in the garden of branching paths has been taken, the course of events will never be able to return to their original route.

The events and people have branched off in a different direction.

Fate decreed that I would walk through the maze blindfold.

Part One

Chapter 1

They shall come back

Harley Street Sept 1992

S "Where are you now Janet?"

"I am waiting to come back."

S "What is it like?"

"A void."

S "How do you feel about coming back?"

"I don't want to come back."

S "Why not?"

"I know my life will be difficult with a lot of suffering"

S "Do you HAVE to come back?"

"Yes I have no choice."

"Something is pulling at me, I don't want to go."

22/5/53 hospital/London

"It's a red head."

"It's a girl."

I was born after a 48 hour labour to a woman, who I was to find out later was seriously mentally disturbed.

Carrying the genes for a cruel illness. My twin had the sense to opt out. Already I had chosen the wrong path.

My fate was sealed.

90% of patients with my disease are female.

The disease is common in women with red hair or a close relative with red hair.

My mother never forgave me for the long labour.

Her answer to any pain was, "If you think that hurts wait until you have a baby."

Well I never had a baby – but it was admitted by the medical profession in 2010 that the pain of advanced interstitial cystitis was comparable to the pain of childbirth. I can well believe it.

From my birth until the age of 5 we lived in Harlesden. My young years were spent often with my paternal grandmother (my mother went straight back to work as soon as I was born) I remember more of the first five years of my life with her rather than with my parents, although my time was spent between the two. We lived in a flat and my paternal grandparents had a house nearby. I had happy memories of spending time with them and the local park and more than anything, being loved.

I was different though and I sensed it early. I had what is called a "gift" of sometimes seeing things before they happened. Usually in dreams but Sometimes I just "knew" things without being able to explain why.

I remember one day I must have been about three at the time, saying to my parents.

"When I grow up I will never get married."

They laughed thinking it was just the thinking of a three year old but I was stating a fact. I KNEW I would never marry.

I then had a recurring dream. I was older, I was somewhere that was not a very nice place. I was afraid. Many years later I realised this was a law court. This has not happened yet but it was on the cards, either I have branched off down another road and avoided it, or it will happen in the future. I will just have to wait and see.

I was clearly loved by all my relatives, I do not remember

being hit or shouted at back then or being given any reason to believe I was not loved by everyone.

Then things changed.

The first was the birth of my brother and the second was that we moved to Kenton, in North London.

My paternal grandmother no longer looked after me.

My mother's habit of shouting orders, her domineering nature and her attitude to children (not just her own but other peoples) began to manifest.

Control freak was a polite way of describing it.

"You are the most rude/dirty/lazy/disobedient/ horrible child it has ever been my misfortune to meet," she would scream at me. (Her experience of children was limited!) "Why can't you be more like J?" J was my friend, she had a sweet innocent look that was very deceptive and fooled many people. I was the opposite. Even from that young age I would stand my corner with her and argue back. It probably helped me to survive. "I'm going to give you a good thrashing," she would shout at me. Even in those days repeatedly shouting at and hitting children was NOT the accepted norm. My relatives never hit or shouted at me, I could not understand why my mother found it necessary to do so. I was an average child my behaviour was average children's, but she seemed to look at me and treat me as something nasty. Someone to take her anger out on. Looking back I cannot work out why no-one in our family tried to intervene, or at least say something to her. I can only conclude that they were in some way afraid of her. No-one ever stood up to her in anything. My father was used by her to correct me.

"Speak to her D," she would order him.

"Do as your mother tells you to," he would shout, accompanied by a blow. Often he did not know what the problem was or why he was hitting me, but my mother had spoken and that was enough, (years later I learned that he wished he had left her and taken me with him.) I found refuge from all this in our local church.

Soon after we had moved to Kenton our neighbour asked my mother if I would like to go to the local Sunday school.

"No," I replied – I had had enough of school – I hated it.

"You're going," said my mother. Not that she had any religious views, it meant I would be out of the house and besides she did not want to upset the neighbours.

So I was sent to Sunday school and fell in love with the place.

No one shouted at me, no one hit me, I felt safe, the other children were kind as were all the teachers.

That church played an important part in my life for the next fifteen years. Not so much because of religion though obviously it played a part but there I felt I belonged, I was as good as the others, people liked me.

I was also a loner. I preferred being on my own, I still do, and I sensed even at that young age that my life was not going to follow the "normal" pattern.

I remember a conversation I had with my friends, we were discussing, as young girls do what we would do when we were grown up. They all said that they would marry and have children. I heard a voice in my mind saying quite clearly, "It will not be that way for you, you will have other things to do with your life."

I had my health. Apart from the odd cold or childhood illness I was fine and of course I accepted this as the way it should be. My mother saw our illnesses as an inconvenience.

During my primary school years if I was ill on a weekday

I was sent to school, and sometimes sent home again.

During my secondary school years I had to show my mother my timetable if it included Maths or English I was sent in.

(It did no good, I am still hopeless at Maths!), and again I was often sent home again.

"Why aren't you at school?" she would snap at me when she returned from work and found me in.

"Got sent home," I would snap back.

Her answer to any illness, pain etc., was you carried on, worked it off, did not give in to it.

Both my grandmothers had strokes, my paternal grandmother recovered after a very long disabling period, with comments from my mother that she could do so much more if she wanted to!

Her own mother had a much more severe stroke and never regained consciousness.

When it came to visiting any relative in hospital or later in a care home my mother's complaint was, "It's such an awkward place to get to."

As if someone had deliberately chosen to be ill or in that particular hospital just to be bloody awkward.

The only time when she DID take an interest in my health was when I needed to visit a dentist.

From a very young age I had had trouble with my teeth.

My first dentist was supposed to be a children's dentist, how he ever got to work with children I will never know.

"Stop making that noise," he would snap if any child dared to cry.

(Knowing what I know now I really had something to cry for.)

My second dentist was kindness itself.

My teeth were very bad, the second ones came through

bad. Lack of calcium was mentioned, but nothing done so the result was many silver fillings.

"Don't worry if you swallow the silver bits," he reassured me as I washed my mouth out. "They are harmless."

Of course I believed him. Nor do I blame him, the dangers of silver fillings were not known then, everyone had them.

At the age of twelve, in the second year of my secondary school I had much dental treatment, and many silver fillings in an effort to "save" my second teeth.

Meanwhile my mother's behaviour was becoming more disturbing – but brought up in that atmosphere day after day, I accepted it although I knew that it was not considered "normal" even by the standards of 1965 it was not acceptable to threaten your children with a stick, or to keep threatening to thrash them.

My mother would sit down to Sunday lunch with a cane in her hand and snap, "The first one to talk gets it!"

Or to keep repeating, "Children should be seen and not heard."

"When I was your age we did not have such and such (so you won't have it either.)

Or to persistently shout orders that she expected us to immediately obey. My friend J said to me that she always knew when I was in as she could hear my mother shouting at me from down the street!

Most of the abuse was levelled at me, first because it was me she hated most (I never found out why) and because I would not take it. I would answer back. I had a strong sense of fairness and justice, and still do.

I will not take being unfairly treated or wrongly accused.

One Sunday after she had again threatened me with the stick (while my father always sat there as if this behaviour was normal) I grabbed the stick from her hand, broke it over my knee, gave her half and said, "There is your half here is mine." I expected either her or my father to retaliate.

Neither did, my father almost grinned, she did nothing, shocked that I had stood up to her, but she never threatened me with a stick again.

It was my first victory.

My second was realising that she liked to see me cry. Like all bullies she liked to see her victims cringe.

One day she shouted, and hit while I watched her face contorted with anger that she could not make me cry. My second victory.

My happiest times were the summer holidays. I often spent up to three weeks staying with relatives during the summer. My maternal grandmother in Wimbledon, a weekend with my great aunt, a week with my paternal grandparents. My brother was too young to come with me. Happy times when it was just me, I was loved, cared for no one shouted at me, hit me, bullied me, or told me I was worthless.

During those long summer holidays and the weekends in Battersea Park when there were pleasure gardens and fun fairs and I was away from my mother and enjoyed for a few weeks what would have been a normal childhood.

Why did I not tell anyone else what was going on? Why did I not speak up?

Well you didn't then, you kept such things to yourself, besides my mother was clever, a good actress. When relatives stayed I was not hit, I was not shouted at, (or not very often) my mother called me "dear". No-one would have believed me. I stayed alive by keeping my mouth shut about what was happening in that house.

I know now there was NOTHING I could have said

or done that would have changed anything – only made it worse.

While I know NOW that my father was not condoning what she was, he wanted to hide it. It has been suggested that he protected me from her. I remember no such protection – only fear.

Chapter 2

Insanity

A winter night. A woman comes into a room, looks at the sleeping child and goes over to the gas fire. Turns on the gas and leaves the child to die. The child wakes up, sees the woman walk out of the room. The child gets up, turns off the gas. She tells no one, she calls no one.

The next morning I told my mother that I had woken up and the gas was on and she replied, "You dreamt it."

I then told my father his reply was, "Oh oh."

The rest of that night until in 1992 when under hypnosis I remembered it, was a blank. I did not know until 1992 that my father had played no part in my attempted murder.

Again I told no one. In those days there was no ChildLine, child abuse was not recognised.

I knew that I would not be believed. Had I told my life would have been hell. She would have stopped at nothing to shut me up.

Even if I HAD been believed nothing would have been done.

My life would have been in further danger.

There was no counselling no excuses such as depression/stress/she needs help or any of the other excuses that, are so common today.

There was no excuse for murder. If I had spoken

out and been believed she would have been put in a psychiatric hospital for MANY years or in prison.

By keeping quiet I took the life sentence that should have been hers.

Her thanks to me for keeping quiet were to tell everyone who would listen.

"Janet imagines things." "We don't know what it is all about."

My one regret for much of my life was that I did not leave that bloody gas on.

My thirteenth year was mostly a happy one.

I was getting too big to hit now, and after the incident with the cane she changed tactic anyway. Realising that blows did not now affect me, the verbal abuse began to get worse.

I had a circle of friends, I spent more time at the church, and away from her and the house. Other people liked me, so why didn't she? I could not be all the things she yelled at me, if I was no one would like me, want to be friends with me, and so it must be her, not me. Consciously I knew this – subconsciously I was not so sure.

One thing that she was obsessed with and always had been was my school work. From when I first began school she would set me work that was far beyond my knowledge and scream at me when I could not do it. When my friends were out playing I was sitting in the dining room trying to work out sums which I usually got wrong and had her screaming – 'why are you so stupid?' Strangely she never did this to my younger brother – who really did not care or try.

Nothing was ever good enough for her. When I moved from my junior school to my senior school I found I had been put in the second A class.

I had never been in an A class before, I was average and

had always been a B. I had achieved something that would actually please her and ran home with the news. Her reply, "It's not good enough you should be in the FIRST A class."

It was a pattern that was to follow me and affect me for many years. Not good enough, no matter how hard I tried it was NEVER good enough.

Well in my thirteenth year I was getting good reports, I had come first in one exam which had pushed up my place from near the bottom of the second A class to the middle. One lesson I loved was biology.

We were learning about the eyes and I must have said something about this to her for she showed me her eyes, and pointed out that the pupil of one of her eyes came to a point at the top instead of being completely round. I thought it was unusual and thought no more about it until 1994 when I studied to become an Iridologist.

The sign is called 'church peak pupil' it is very rare and is seen in the eyes of someone who is seriously mentally disturbed, or psychotic.

I was beginning to grow up now, and I began thinking that life would not always be like this. One day I suppose I would work, move away, be happy. Having a boyfriend or getting married were not in my dreams or in my plans, in fact the very thought either repulsed me or I felt nothing. But I did not have to worry yet. In two years I assumed I would have a boyfriend simply because then I would be 15 and everyone had one.

Now I did not understand the attraction that my friends had.

"Isn't he lovely, I saw him today, he SPOKE to me." This left me cold, which was fortunate. It could never be anyway. The first visible signs of my disease were about to start.

The only reason I went to a doctor was that I had a pain in my right side and my mother thought it might be my appendix.

"It's more likely to be her kidneys," said Dr D. "I will do some tests."

I was only vaguely aware of what kidneys were for and the role they played and how they worked. Apart from needing to use a toilet more often than was average and having done so all my life, I had never been ill or showed any sign of kidney disease. The tests showed albumin in my urine. Now this is a danger sign that should have been immediately picked up, alarm bells should have started ringing. Instead Dr D. decided that this was normal and as I was not ill or in pain and hated the tests, and was a thirteen year old who hadn't a clue what was going on so I was relieved when he said there was nothing wrong and forgot about it for years.

Looking back of course now in 2011 it was obvious that the 'harmless' silver fillings I had the year before had already started to do damage, the kidneys were working hard to throw off the poison and this was what was causing the problem.

I do not have the notes from that time, they were destroyed long ago, but I often ask myself how the hell the NHS could in its incompetence have ignored the fact that since the age of thirteen I had kidney problems and not connected them to cystitis. It beggars belief.

The pain stopped, there were no more tests after that year and I forgot about it. The verbal abuse worsened. I continued to keep quiet about it – who could I tell? My own father did nothing, said nothing, ignored it and as far as I knew then, condoned it. I almost lived a double life – outside I was quiet, polite, shy, and seemingly well liked by everyone except my mother.

In my early teens we went around in groups with my other girlfriends – my mother continually nagged me, "When are you going to get a boyfriend?" This had began at the age of 11 and was now getting worse. All my friends were pairing off with boys, saying how wonderful boys were – apart from a few minor crushes on boys, I felt nothing and did not want to – the whole thing left me cold.

Yet at the same time she did not want me to grow up – afraid that she would lose the control over me. My grandmother joined in the when are you going to get a boyfriend game, then on the odd occasion when we met for family gatherings the same from female relatives. Obviously I had been discussed and found wanting.

My father and my other relatives did not mention it – the obsession was on my mother's side.

Now I know that the reason I felt nothing was part of the disease, mercury interferes with the hormones, the body produces them but the mercury interferes with their action. Which is why I felt nothing.

I was already ill, then the first symptoms that the rest of my urinary tract had become involved had began.

At first it was just a form of mild inflammation of the urethra, a bit annoying but nothing to worry about. The only reason I went to my GP was that we were due to go on holiday.

A test showed I had UTI and I was given Ampicillin to treat it.

As the symptoms did not clear completely I was given a second prescription for Ampicillin. Again it did not clear completely but there was no pain, I did not feel unwell, and I assumed it would clear up on its own. I had had similar milder symptoms for many years, not knowing what they were and they cleared. I now know I was born with kidney disease.

Meanwhile at home the atmosphere was worsening.

"Why don't you go out and get pregnant, or get hooked on drugs? At least you would be normal!" my mother screamed at me.

There were frequent rows, not just because I was growing up but because I was not growing up to be a clone of my mother.

She had married had 2 children, worked in an office, I was going to be the same.

Her anger, her control was worsening and I knew now I had to get away from home. Unfortunately her continual 'you are rubbish' attitude had done its work. I was afraid that life outside would be worse, I had no confidence, it was a case of the hell I knew was better than the one I did not. My father said and did nothing. I was stuck in a catch-22.

By this time I had left college and was working as a temp, in an office in Pinner. There were three women in this office and they had bitching down to a fine art. When one of them left the office the other two would start to talk about her. One day one of them told her colleague that the other lady had had an operation to remove her bladder and had to wear a bag. Now here was I, with a disease with no name but loosely called cystitis, to give it one no idea when I was going to get well or how, it was just what I needed to hear. I could not have imagined anything worse or sick than to walk around like that. How does any woman live like that, a mutilated freak – I would rather be dead than live like that! Had I known then that many years later I would be begging a surgeon to remove my bladder to end the pain and illness I would probably have ended my life.

I was still going to the church – a peaceful haven to home. Church Sunday morning, home to lunch and the 'control freak' church in the evening. Then the beginning of a turning point.

"We are moving to Devon," my mother announced.

"We are going to run a bed and breakfast hotel, N you are going to be a waiter, Janet you are going to be a cleaner.

"Am I hell," was my reply, (my brother just sat there and took it all – he hardly ever answered back).

"Well I thought you would not like to wait at table," she replied after she had got over the shock that I had refused.

"Did it ever occur to you that I may have plans of my own, that I may not want to work for YOU?" I replied.

Her face made it clear that NO she had not thought – I was going to do as I was told, "Well if that's your attitude," she snapped.

My father spoke then.

"It's your life and your decision," he said. One of the few times he had openly taken my side against her.

I knew then I had to leave, had to get out. I had this mental picture of me being dragged to Devon, and working for her and putting up with her madness for the rest of my life. Things were going to change.

My mind wanted to get out, my body put plans on hold.

I was starting to lose weight my disease was worsening, further tests kept showing I had UTI, I was given further antibiotics and due to the atmosphere at home I was now on antidepressants.

I knew I was physically ill but my GP did not think of sending me to hospital or taking it further.

I was nearly 20, my dentist finally told me that my teeth were all rotten and I should have them all removed and have dentures. At that age it was one of the most devastating pieces of news I had ever heard.

I was a young girl and I would have false teeth and be like an old woman. No one would want to love me.

My teeth were removed including the old fillings, all but three teeth.

One of them containing an old silver filling, and in my blissful ignorance I honestly believed having my teeth removed was the worst thing that could happen.

Finally after 2 years of continual infections my GP sent me to Northwick Park Hospital – then supposed to be the most up to date hospital in the country.

It was now Oct 73 and from the notes I now have it was proved that I had right sided renal angled pain, blood in the urine and was given a cystoscopy (examination of the bladder under anaesthetic.)

Which showed trigonitis (inflammation of the trigone area of the bladder), streptococcal infection was found for which I was given antibiotics.

Now to anyone with ANY medical knowledge this was proof that my disease was physical, in fact anyone with any commonsense could have worked this out!

Our next holiday was in the Isle of Man and soon after arrival I became ill with an appalling migraine and my kidney symptoms had worsened.

To my mother's disgust (we don't have time for this on holiday) I consulted a GP told him what was wrong and showed him some medicine I had been given by my GP.

"This rubbish won't help you," he said. "You have pyelitis, it is dangerous, you need to go into hospital straight away." I explained we were on holiday, he replied, "Well go as soon as you get back, you are VERY ill."

If only I had listened. If only I had gone against

her and walked into a hospital would my life have been different? – maybe not, I will never know. "You are not ruining our holiday," she snapped at me.

So on our return I went back to my GP and told him what had occurred – he would not listen.

Meanwhile my mother was busy telling everyone there was nothing wrong with me. "It's all in her head."

"She has had all the tests, there is nothing wrong with her," she would say to anyone who asked. I had not had ALL the tests I had had a FEW tests and they had showed something WAS wrong. Meanwhile I was losing weight and people were commenting.

"How is your sister?"

"Is Janet OK she looks ill?"

"She is fine, fine," he trilled – he had been told to hide the fact I was ill.

(I never found out why!)

Meanwhile I was sick of the suggestion that my disease was 'all in the mind' and set out to prove it.

I consulted a psychiatrist at Wembley Hospital to prove my disease was physical.

"Why are you wasting my time? You have a kidney disease. I will send you to a kidney specialist at University College Hospital London." At last someone in the medical profession had stated the blindingly obvious. Someone believed I was ill, someone was going to do something, I was going to get well. It would soon be over and I could get on with my life, leave home, have a career I wanted, (not one that my mother wanted me to have), I would have my health back.

It would all soon end.

It was almost heaven.

NO

This was not the end but a beginning. A beginning of a nightmare that was to ruin my health and life, take me to the depths of a hell that no religion could dream of and take nearly 30 years from my life.

And all because a consultant got his facts wrong, wrote defamatory statements on my notes and ensured that I would never be taken seriously by any member of the medical profession.

Ironically now in 2011, I was told by ladies in my IC group that I was then running that UCH has one of the best urological teams in the country. (Obviously I was born at the wrong time!)

Interlude

Before going any further I would like to explain the following.

I had not told anyone about my mother's bizarre behaviour, nor about the attempted murder, nor the mental and physical abuse, or the fact that for the last two years I had slept with a sharp pair of scissors under my pillow to protect myself if she attacked me again, nor of the nightmares that I had had since I was 17 that I had woken up when I had not, a dream within a dream, I now know was a reaction to the attempted murder.

Had these facts been known to the NHS then I could understand how mistakes could have been made, they were NOT known.

And if they were – is this really an excuse for mistaking a serious physical disease for an 'imaginary one?'

So I was due to go to a hospital in London, where clever doctors would sort out what was wrong. That was what I assumed would happen.

From an early age I learned that if you are ill you went to a doctor. This nice clever man would give you medicine and you would get well. If he could not make you well then he sent you to hospital where an even cleverer man called a specialist would make you well, giving you an operation if necessary. It was that straightforward. Yes, there was the odd case where mistakes were made, where people had to return to hospital for another operation to correct the first one, but they were rare.

Everyone believed the doctor knew what he was doing. Did as they were told. Never questioned. What amazes me now in 2011 is that some people still DO.

Also as I had been taught in church God answered all prayers – I had been praying for over two years to be well. No one had explained what was wrong, I was afraid, – because I now had something that was affecting the lower half of my body – and a mother who was convinced it was because I was somehow dirty it had to be hidden away. I knew now what was happening of course. God tested people, he was testing my faith. Because my greatest fear was going into a National Health Hospital – it still is! I had to go through this to get well, then everything would be OK.

Looking back I can laugh now. Back then I really believed this.

Two things happened before the appointment. The first was that one evening my friend was with me at my home and I was in pain, ill and passing blood. My friend went down to my mother and told her.

She looked her straight in the face and replied, "There is nothing wrong with Janet she imagines it."

My friend who knew my mother well and was not very happy with the reply told her mother, who met my father in the street and said to him, "Isn't it time one of you took an interest in your daughter?" (or words to that effect, which my father later told me.)

His reaction was to say to my mother, "When Janet goes for that hospital appointment you go with her."

Two weeks before the appointment my body began to fill with fluid and my abdomen began to swell and swell, until I looked heavily pregnant. (There was no pain whatsoever.)

I phoned UCH and was told to come up to casualty straight away.

Once there I was examined. The doctor refused to believe I was not pregnant at first, finally admitting there was no foetus the swelling was fluid.

No apology.

Then he realised that the swelling around the abdomen was an over dilated bladder. He also told me I had very strong bladder muscles. He inserted a catheter (eventually) it was almost impossible, the pain was horrendous, he refused to stop and I heard the nurse say, "She is going to pass out."

"Let her," he snapped. When I came round two nurses were holding me down. Many years later I learned that I should have had a local anaesthetic.

I was told I had a severe prolonged kidney infection, it was dangerous, it MUST be treated. I must come into hospital for tests.

At last – someone was going find out what was wrong, I was going to get well, get my life back.

That was September 1974 – I got my life back in August 2000.

The NHS took over twenty-five years of it.

So to UCH 10th September 1974 – a date I will NEVER forget.

I had to drag my mother there … She did not want to come in with me. "Ask him if I can come in with you."

"You're coming in." I had come this far, my mother was going to learn I was really ill and not making it up.

The consultant did not have the notes from the previous visit.

He implied I had never been near the hospital.

He examined me quickly, ignored me, looked straight at my mother and said, "Your daughter's disease is in her mind."

And she sat there and said nothing.

Now I am not often lost for words but I was then.

I was disgusted and angry. Red hot angry.

I knew she hated me but to sit there and listen to this crap was low even for her. We did not speak on the way home, on arrival she said, "Well that's it then."

"What do you mean – that's it then?"

"There is nothing wrong with you, you imagine it."

This defamatory rubbish he wrote on my notes. He denied it. In 2002 I legally proved he had lied. The lie was passed from hospital to hospital. Never again would I be taken seriously. Because of one man's incompetence and lies I was branded a 'nutter' by the NHS.

This lie prevented me receiving the treatment I needed. This lie ruined my health and life. It took EIGHTEEN hospitals and many many appointments before the mistake was rectified and I was given my life back. And all the lies and incompetence uncovered.

The NHS have never openly admitted they were wrong, my notes have never been corrected, I have never received any compensation.

I went straight back to the psychiatrist at Wembley.

"What the hell is going on?" I asked. "Can't you write a letter confirming my disease is physical so when I go to my next hospital I don't meet up with another brain dead idiot?"

"I am not allowed to do that," he replied.

"Why not?"

He did not answer.

So I left, went out to find another doctor with a brain cell between the ears. Unaware that I had been branded a 'head case' for LIFE.

Unaware it would take 26 years.

Thank God I never was to know, how long it would be, how much of my life it would take.

Well on arriving home on 10th September 1974 my mother promptly told my father I 'imagined' my disease and of course we all had a massive row. He threatened me with violence because I would not agree with the my crazy mother that my disease was 'all in my head.'

To crown it all my mother threatened to phone a psychiatrist and have me sectioned! The phrase pot and kettle springs to mind!

Yes it is true. Nutty X the child-killer threatened to section ME, if it was not so weird it would have been funny. So now the lunatics were taking over the asylum.

I had a choice, leave Marat Sade or end up inside.

The next day I arranged to move in with a friend.

"I have found somewhere to live and I will be leaving," I announced.

It was the only time I have EVER seen my mother lost for words.

So I left home on 21st September 1974. I was 21, if I had the courage to leave at 18 my life would have been so different.

Chapter 3

Into the unknown

The last two years had damaged me mentally and emotionally far greater than I could imagine, I was to carry the scars for many years. I spent a month living with a good friend who knew a bit about my background and the way I had been treated. I then had to leave and was thrown in at the deep end in a house share with three other girls.

I was also looking for a doctor with a brain who could sort out what was wrong with me. I was now wearing maternity clothes often as I was so swollen with fluid. Also having what I did not know then but learned later were kidney infections as well as the 'cystitis' thankfully not yet bad pain, that came later but obviously ill.

I went to the local health centre and explained that the last doctor I had had was not very good and could I please see one who knew what he was doing, as I had been ill for a long time and wanted things sorted out.

Dr. Noade was not too happy at what the receptionist had told him – so why did she tell him? My reward for daring to ask to see a doctor who knew what he was doing was for him to write to another hospital consultant, and tell him I had a 'longstanding personality disorder was convinced I had some major urinary disorder, and was clinging to the belief that it was physical.'

So now a doctor (not a psychiatrist) has decided I

am mental, added this defamatory comment to my notes (without my knowledge), this is what happens when in 1975 you complain about another doctor.

Unfortunately I did not know this until May 2002 when I saw the notes. My friend who is a qualified psychotherapist found it amusing and said, "Well, you certainly do not have that."

What I DID have was a major urinary disorder and I clung to that belief because it was TRUE.

Meanwhile I was trying to break away from my crazy family, or at least my mother.

I had had enough of being branded looney by my family, it was enough that the medical profession thought I was nuts.

My mother had done NOTHING whatsoever to help or support me, neither had my father, although to give him his due he did not go around saying I 'imagined' my disease.

So I tried to make the break permanent – after all my mother obviously hated me and I thought she would be happy if we never met again.

The result was a very long sixteen page letter A4 size which she did not send to me but to my Great Aunt. God knows why, listing every 'imaginary' fault she could think of. My Aunt sent it to me (I've no idea why, most people would have thrown it into the dustbin!) I showed it to one of the girls I was sharing a house with and she said, "Your mother is not all there."

Well I knew that, but for the first time in my life someone actually SAID it. These letters followed a pattern (and not only letters to me.)

It seemed if I ever tried to break contact all the hatred came out in letters (the second one had only 8 pages.) I could not understand it, the woman hated me from the day

I was born, why did she want to cling onto me why did she not just tell me to bog off?

She then accused me of phoning her and slamming the phone down when she answered. When I confronted her with it and asked, "How do you know it was me if the person (if they exist) slams the phone down when you pick it up?"

"It's an office background I can hear," she replied.

I pointed out that there were offices all over the country and why would I bother to phone someone I did not want any contact with, I asked.

She had no reply to that but when I tried again a few years later to break off the verbal abuse began again.

She hated me but would not openly admit it.

She would not let go, she still wanted to hurt and bully and control, and kept up the 'My daughter imagines things' 'We don't know what it is all about.'

By now I was beginning to experience minor gynecological problems, thrush discharges etc both as a reaction to the change in the gut bacteria due to the antibiotics I was taking (for the infection that did not officially exist because I imagined it) and also the 'imaginary' infection when not treated will of course spread.

I discovered the world of 'special clinics' then a fancy word for a VD clinic but they also treated similar non-sexual infections.

Now I learned a lot from these clinics.

1. USUALLY I was taken seriously, told I had UTI and given antibiotics.
2. Not to say I had never had sex because they thought you were a bit weird if you did.

3. That what I had was called (loosely) cystitis. It was nothing to do with sex, it was an infection, quite common and of course it was REAL not 'imaginary', not psychological, but PHYSICAL.

Now there were some exceptions. I soon learned not to go to the same one TWICE if I wanted to be taken seriously, as the clinic doctors contacted your GP and I knew although I could not prove it and it had been strenuously denied, that my notes held untrue and defamatory statements but they were certainly more use over the years than hospital consultants.

Now in June 1975 I believed at last I had made a breakthrough.

I was given a referral to St Peter's Hospital London then the best teaching hospital for kidney disease. They will sort it out – I was told.

Wrong again.

Following an IVP, (kidney X-ray) a cystoscopy (internal examination of my bladder) and one negative MSU test I was told there was nothing wrong with me I 'imagined' my disease, I needed a psychiatrist. How did the top teaching hospital in the country make such a stupid mistake? Why was he allowed to practice if he was so incompetent and how many more women's lives did he ruin?

We will never know. In 2002 when the truth was discovered and it was legally proved that Mr C and St Peter's hospital was the main culprit in my wrong diagnosis he had by then died.

Which was fortunate for him – had he been alive I would have told him what I thought of him.

Meanwhile I was moving around London from flat to bedsit, now living in Rayners Lane with two of the girls from the original house share, and out of the blue, by chance I saw a woman GP.

You are very ill, she informed me, you need to go to hospital to get this checked out I will write you a letter.

Brilliant – here was my mistake, seeing MEN doctors, women were more intelligent. I do not remember what happened exactly only that I never got to hospital and if I did nothing was done, all I remember about this time was that I had been doing everything wrong it was simple – find a FEMALE consultant – there was the answer.

Meanwhile it was suggested that I might get on better if I paid. Things move when you pay I was told so I consulted a private GP, Dr

MJ in Kenton. Now having lived in Kenton for sixteen years I had passed this man's house many times – my mistake was not passing it this time!

MJ examined me – obviously unknown to me he had read the lies on my notes and sent me to his colleague in Harley Street.

Harley Street – the street of the best doctors in the country. At last.

I should have gone there in the first place. How much time had I wasted with NHS doctors when there was Harley Street.

Expensive but this would sort out my health, give me my life and health back. Dreaming is free!

Now Dr R, I was told was a DOCTOR I only discovered in 2002 that he was actually a psychiatrist.

He gave me some little yellow tablets, told me they were antibiotics and I should take three a day.

He charged me £21.00 which in those days was exorbitant.

For three days I walked around in a complete fog, the

tablets made me so dopey I did not know or care what day it was and it was a horrible unpleasant dopey but I had paid £21.00 for these wonderful antibiotics from a Harley Street doctor so I must put up with it. I was going to get well.

Three days later I went down to a healer in Sussex (who became a good friend) had a cheese salad for lunch and started to develop a bad headache.

Now normally with a bad headache I would have taken paracetamol etc but B was a healer so not wishing to be rude I stuck it out.

The headache became much more severe, so B phoned her friend P who was a nursing sister who came round and asked me if I was on any medication I showed her the 'antibiotics' she phoned a colleague and asked him what these were.

Next she made me sick, then I woke up hours later and B told me, "You nearly died."

The 'antibiotics' were strong antidepressants which should not be mixed with certain foods including cheese and he had told me to take three times the normal dosage.

The headache was a warning that I was heading for a brain haemorrhage my blood pressure had gone sky high. If P had not made me sick I would not now be writing this book.

On returning to London furious that I had actually PAID this quack as much as anything I complained to MJ.

His reply was that if I said anything to anyone he would have me sectioned. Now of course I know this was only a threat, I should have reported both DR R and MJ.

In those days it would not have done any good. Doctors were then always believed over patients.

Again in 2002 it was proved that Dr R had written on my notes that my frequency and cystitis were due to 'hysteria'. He also describes me as a woefully inadequate personality – not bad for a 'doctor' who saw me once for less than an hour and then nearly killed me!

So now here was I believing that things could not get any worse but at least I knew where I was going wrong now.

I needed to be treated by a woman, I needed a woman friend, I knew now my disease was purely physical, I knew I was very ill. I believed that as soon as I found the right person things would be all right – I would get well, be happy have my life back.

It was now February 76 – thirty-six years later as I write this I find it hard to believe that I thought it was so simple, that I was so naive.

That I thought that one day these quacks would see the blindingly obvious.

They never have – perhaps they never will.

Interlude

Looking back, was there anything I could have done that would have changed the future?

I believe not.

Fate had dealt me a rotten hand.

I played it the best way I could.

I was born at a time when no-one questioned doctors, when child abuse was not recognised (and if it was things were hidden.)

Born into a family that did not care, to a woman who was psychotic. Treated by a medical profession which was ignorant and blind, wrongly branded hysterical/woefully inadequate personality/personality disordered/with a fantastic 'imagination' and come through it alive and still sane I feel I have coped pretty well!

My life was now a round of work, come home from work, go to bed, why? Because now as well as the 'cystitis' that did not officially exist I was exhausted with lack of sleep, and by now the discomfort and illness was added pain. Pelvic pain that dragged and dragged me down with it. Low back pain and abdominal pain. I came home from work stayed in bed clutching a hot water bottle, tried to sleep got up the next morning and went into work and carried on as usual. Why? Because I HAD to, because no one would believe I was ill, because my disease had to be hidden. Women did not openly talk of pelvic pain, of cystitis, or anything similar. No one wanted to know or listen. Anyway I 'imagined' I was ill.

This pattern of coming home and spending the evenings in bed went on for many months I was now 22. Most twenty-two year olds were dating, getting married, having a good time, furthering their career. If they were ill then someone family or friend would be helping them, they would be in hospital they would be getting treatment. Someone would be caring for them, someone would be sympathetic, someone would be asking why nothing was being done, someone would be fighting for them. I had none of this.

My illness must be hidden away.

Still determined that I WAS going to get to the bottom of what was wrong with me, I found my way to St Paul's Hospital London.

Here at last the truth was discovered – and promptly 'lost.'

"You have a prolonged untreatable infection in the kidneys," I was told. "You will spend the rest of your life on antibiotics and pain killers. There is nothing we can do."

My first question was typical me. "How the hell had the

NHS got it so wrong, why was it not discovered, and why had I been lied to?"

His reply was, "It's not this hospital it was someone else."

"You are still the NHS, sort it."

So what happens now I asked.

"Your kidneys will eventually fail, there is nothing we can do, come back when you are dying and we will put you on a kidney machine but there is nothing we can do to stop your disease getting to that point."

The fact that I was going to die did not worry me too much.

At least the pain and illness was going to end.

At least I had proof my disease was REAL.

(I remained on antibiotics on repeat prescription for a total of NINETEEN years for an infection that was never admitted to officially exist.)

There are no records of this consultation.

When in 2002 my solicitor was tracing the notes for legal action it was found that two years of the notes from September 1975 to January 1977 were 'missing'.

So I was going to die – thank God an end to it.

I did not tell anyone – why?

Because I doubted anyone would believe me.

Now all I wanted to do was die and get away from pain and illness and if I told anyone they may try to stop it happening and who did I tell.

My family believed I was mental, or most of them did!

I was so ill and in pain that any social life was almost impossible.

The idea even of any relationship was a joke, even if I had wanted one which then it was the last thing I needed or wanted.

So I decided to spend the last few years of my life, on my own, quietly just going to work, coming home, spending my evenings in bed.

Far from being bad for me, it kept me sane, helped me cope and then and now I realise it was the sensible thing to do.

Then in February 1976 my life again took a wrong turning.

Chapter 4

Taking Over the Asylum

The most dangerous people in the world are those who THINK they know what is better for other people.

If I was given the chance to change one moment in my life it would be to have turned back and not walked up that path and met T.

Yet it was just what I was looking for. A bed-sitter in a shared house, near work, cheap, nice landlady who was away most of the time anyway, a chance to either sort out my health, or die, whichever happened I did not really care but I was not going to continue to live in limbo.

How wrong I was. T was to turn my life into a living hell.

When I finally got away eight years later only then could I look back and see her for the sick, deluded and dangerous woman she was and think why had I not made more effort to get away, just cut my losses and left. My only excuse was that then I believed I had not long to live, I was too ill, did not have the gumption, and I truly believed she would see how wrong she was – she never did.

This woman offered me something I had never had from my family. Affection, interest and I believed I had met the person who was to help me get well, support me, and give me back my life. I realise now that if I had not been so strong she would have taken my sanity.

"You will be lucky if you see 25," my new GP told me.

I walked out of that surgery on air. I was 23. Only another 2 years of hell and I would be released. Only another 2 years of illness and pain. Spending Saturday mornings in that surgery waiting for more antibiotics for my 'imaginary' disease – I had just heard the best news of my life.

I had finally got free from my last GP who was convinced my disease was 'all in my head' (well he had read my notes hadn't he!)

And met this lovely man who said to me, "I can't do anymore for you but I hope you find someone who can."

He lived up to his name Dr Goodman – who was one of the few people in the medical world I trusted and respected and one of the few who was honest.

Sadly, soon after that he died of cancer – the world lost a good doctor.

So things were not too bad. I was going to die, I had made friends with the couple in the top flat. Work was bearable – just – I took each day as it came put up with the pain, and feeling ill.

Told no one how ill I felt because on the odd occasion when I had spoken out and said I was ill or in pain the usual remark was – well at least you don't have cancer, (so it doesn't matter does it.)

I had learned by now that keeping quiet was the best option.

I was seeing B (my friend the healer) often. Just spending time with her, being allowed to say I was ill, and in pain, being with someone who understood and cared. The healing made no difference, but it did not matter. Other people had been healed (I had met them) and the belief kept me alive and sane.

Meanwhile my parents were planning to move to Devon still.

Although I had made it clear I would never live with them in Devon. I had moved, got away, why the hell should I go back to a woman who hated me and told everyone I was crazy!

Of course my disease was still 'all in my head'.

Finally she screamed at me, "Yes you ARE ill but you will never get well."

Now I have never believed in curses but this sounded very much like one. What sort of mother says that to her daughter? – I suppose the sort who tries to kill her daughter, abuses her daughter, hates her daughter – stupid question.

"Then I will never come to Devon to visit you," I told her.

And apart from one time in 1984 – my brother's wedding I never did. Friends, other relatives who went to visit told me they were living in the back of beyond, all right for a holiday but too quiet, they would not like to live there. Why did I not visit? – they could not understand it. My parents wanted me to go, they missed me.

The 'I do not know what it is all about' syndrome – continued until her death in 1997.

My new landlady was kind to me, and I was slowly getting to know her. One day when I did a little shopping for her a lady who ran the local shop warned me, "Be careful of T, she will take over your life."

This did not worry me. I wanted someone to take over my life, I wanted someone to care, I wanted someone to take control and help me fight.

My mistake was choosing the wrong person.

Still dragging myself home from work and spending most of the evenings in bed trying to cope with the pain, having no life other than work (why it never occurred to me then to give up work as anyone else would in my condition I did not know) partly because my disease did not show, so of course to others it did not exist and partly because deep down I knew the NHS were not going to do anymore so private treatment was the only option.

So I took myself off to Harley Street again and consulted a doctor who as luck would have it had a brother who was a urologist, who agreed to see me on the NHS.

So in January 1977 I arrived at the West Berks Hospital Reading for a cystoscopy (my third) and other tests.

On arrival I was told that there was no bed for me. Now this was long before it became necessary to phone your hospital on the day of admission to check if there was still a bed – to turn up and find there was not was then unheard of.

Furious that I would be treated in this way – even by the NHS! – I refused to leave the hospital until they found me one.

I was given a bed in a very large half empty geriatric ward – and an apology.

The result of the cystoscopy was trigonitis again – which I learned can only be present if there has been infection and also consistent with both acute and chronic cystitis. So it DID exist.

The consultant confirmed that my disease was NOT psychological and furthermore – not found out until I saw my notes in 2002, a mass had been found in my abdomen, it was smooth and hard 3cm. I was never told, this was never investigated.

Well I am still alive so I assume it was non malignant!

So confident that YET AGAIN it had been confirmed my disease was physical I believed for a little while that perhaps I was not going to die.

My feelings on this were mixed.

Soon after this, although the healing was not helping my physical condition it was keeping me sane, I learned the name of a psychic surgeon, being the type of person who will not give up and try anything once I travelled down from London to Red Hill after work one day to see the famous psychic surgeons the Souters.

Obviously I told no one again – it was enough I was seeing a healer – a psychic surgeon – more evidence Janet has lost the plot.

Now a lot of rubbish has been written about psychic surgery – usually saying it is faked.

What happened that evening could not in any way have been faked and I have never been able to explain it.

This man had never heard of me, never met me, and did not ask me what was wrong.

He simply asked me to lay down on the bench and held his hands over my body.

"There is an obstruction in your abdomen and that is what is causing the trouble," he said.

"You will not be well until it is removed and it will be a long time before it is."

He was 100% right – the obstruction – my bladder was removed in 2000 Twenty-three years later.

Some things cannot be explained, obviously there are forces we cannot understand. There are more things in Heaven and earth.

This renewed my belief in healing, (even if it did not work for me).

I am only thankful he did not tell me how long the 'long time' was.

Meanwhile my new landlady and I got to know each other, often staying up late and talking, she seemed to care, I told her about my crazy mother and the way she had treated me. I spent Sundays with her, she seemed kind and caring, she seemed to understand I was ill and in pain.

And while someone was bothered it all seemed bearable. I began to believe I would one day be well. Began to think – when I am well instead of if.

The dying processes seemed to have stopped. Yes I was often ill with kidney infections – which no one connected with cystitis for some bizarre reason. I was swallowing pain killers and antibiotics continually, which did not seem to bother a medical profession who were willing to give them to me for a condition which supposedly did not exist.

I hated the antibiotics but they did knock the edge off the symptoms and every time I tried to stop them the infection ran riot and I felt so ill I went back on them, and so the pattern continued.

No one questioning why a woman of 24 was living on painkillers and antibiotics for a condition that was not supposed to exist, no one questioning why I was so thin, why my body kept swelling with fluid, why I kept getting kidney infections why I had continual cystitis.

And always being told – well you haven't got cancer so what is the problem?

Meanwhile things were beginning slowly to change.

Twelve years earlier my landlady had had a nervous breakdown and spent 6 months in a psychiatric hospital. Now this was no secret, she had told me not long after she first met me – in fact she told everyone, it was almost as if she was proud of it.

This was at a time when if anyone had had any form of mental illness they kept quiet about it, so I did think this was a bit strange. Everything was 'before my breakdown' or 'after my breakdown.'

This did not worry me too much, she seemed a normal

sensible kind woman and what ever had happened she was obviously OK now. Now knowing that people who are mentally unbalanced can appear perfectly normal, I realise I should have been more careful. But someone cared about me, someone was taking an interest in me, and to be honest I was enjoying it. After over twenty years of indifference, of being told I was nothing, someone cared. If it hadn't been for my being so ill I could have described it as perfect happiness.

The only flaw was that she loved parties – I hated them – I still do.

She could not get her head round this and just accept it. Each year she had a large party on her birthday. Each year I dreaded it. She would just not accept I was not the party type, and on this evidence alone she based the idea that I was 'sick.'

Now I had never heard the word 'sick' used to describe mental illness. Sick to me meant vomit throw up, or physically ill. So when I heard her having the following conversation with the lady in the top flat I just assumed she was telling her I was physically ill.

"Janet is sick."

"Yes, she has a kidney disease."

"No..." the rest I did not hear.

Had I been a little wiser alarm bells would have started to ring. They didn't. Or perhaps subconsciously I chose not to hear them.

Apart from being so ill it was the happiest I had ever been in my life.

I was away from my mother, I had my own home. One day I believed or had started to believe I would be well. Or dead. Either way I would be out of this hellish disease.

Things were slowly changing, and I did not see the

signs, I was too busy in my own world where at last someone cared about me.

People had breakdowns, people got over them. Slowly she got a hold over me. Slowly the truth came out, and I was so blind it is only now over thirty years later I see just how dangerous she was.

No- one around her must be unhappy. No one around her must be depressed for any reason. Everyone she knew needed 'help', everyone she knew was 'sick.' By now I knew what she meant by the word 'sick' and I ignored it, because I knew she had got it wrong, because I knew I was physically ill, and assumed that in the fullness of time when it was discovered I was physically ill everything would be all right.

It was now July 1977 and I was back in St Peter's (obviously the first time was not enough for me) at last we began to discover that something was wrong. E. coli infection was found (I was told the test was clear).

Also trigonitis (I was told everything was normal, nothing found.) sent home then ended up in St Paul's Hospital the next day and told I should never have been discharged from St Peter's.

The consultant at St Paul's told me he would phone St Peter's and ask them to take me straight back.

"God knows why they let you out, you are clearly ill," he told me.

So he phoned St Peter's who refused to take me back, stating that there was nothing wrong with me. The consultant at St Paul's was surprised (I wasn't) kept me in that night then I went home. Still none the wiser as to what had been found, until May 2002 when the truth came to light.

Three months later I was back in St Peter's.

One of the questions I was asked around this time and many times after was had I ever had radiation treatment for cancer, or had I ever had TB. No-one would explain WHY I was being asked this. I now know that both radiation treatment and TB can cause IC.

While in hospital I had a another cystoscopy, my fourth, a bladder biopsy, chronic inflammatory cells were found in the deeper layer of the bladder wall, the bladder was inflamed and scarred, and the consultant had written on the notes that IC was a possibility.

I also had a urethral dilation, my second or third – a treatment that even then was known to be outdated and useless.

The consultant had written in the notes that there was no record of the result of the biopsy. Ignored the fact that I could have IC. I was told there was nothing wrong, and a month later a consultant told me my symptoms were 'all in my head' and tried to put me on valium.

I tore up the prescription in front of him and told him where to stick his valium. I KNEW I was physically ill.

Meanwhile the happy times in Wembley were about to end.

Each year T and her husband K would spend three months in Spain, three in England, three in Spain etc. I looked after their flat, collected the rents, and up to now we had got on fine. Then on return from Spain T's whole personality had changed. I don't know who she had spoken to, or what they had said, or what had caused this.

I was 'sick' because I did not believe my disease was psychological. I was 'sick' because I could not cope with parties. I was 'sick' because I did not go out and meet people.

The fact that I was very ill, at times in almost unbearable pain, was not taken into consideration. It did not exist or it was nothing much. She had decided I was a 'head case.' If I showed ANY negative emotion I was labelled 'sick.'

So I learned to hide how I felt. Learned to hide the pain, learned to pretend. Learned to lie. That pleased her.

During this period I discovered Alternative/ Complementary medicine, (which then was still seen as fringe medicine), and I did it on the quiet. The three months when they were away in Spain I would see complementary therapists, the three months she was here I would stop.

Looking back it seems strange but I was trapped in a situation with a strange, strong-minded woman who was convinced I was crazy and wanted to 'help' me. It took all I had to get through a days work (I never considered giving up work.) There was no-one to keep me, my family had not wanted to know, no-one would employ me, I was too ill, and I must not of course say I was ill because my illness did not officially exist and the lower half of my body was involved and we don't talk about that do we. Pelvic pain does not officially exist.

Then in March 1978 back to Wembley hospital. Not the best place to be. The first thing I was told in the urology dept in March 1978 was, "Back in 1974 you saw a psychiatrist here, didn't you?"

"Yes, that is right, he sent me to UCH because there was nothing wrong with me."

The last part of the sentence was ignored – I had seen a psychiatrist, I was labelled. The fact it had been over 4 years ago, and he said I was normal was ignored. And was ignored for nearly 18 years.

I have never really understood how in nearly 30 years this one part of my notes was always found, while others more up to date that stated I was PHYSICALLY ill had always mysteriously disappeared.

Well the urologist there said it was not their problem, I needed a gynecologist as I now had gynecological problems (infections that are not treated spread) in June at the same hospital the gynecologist said it was a urology problem and sent me back to urology and then in December 1978 the urologist decided it was 'all in my head' there was nothing wrong with me! At no point did anyone have the sense to treat or even investigate both sets of symptoms together, or even recognise that there was a connection.

Well this was the NHS!

Also in that year in April 1978 I went back to the Royal Free Berks as my faith in Wembley was at its lowest – can you blame me.

By now I had had enough and I asked Dr L to perform a cystectomy (bladder removal.)

My worst nightmare come true but that is how low I felt. A woman of 25 and I was asking a consultant to remove my bladder I was so sick of my disease.

"There is no such operation," he told me.

So I was still being treated as the village idiot by the NHS.

"I know someone who has had one," I told him.

"Well it is not appropriate for you," was his reply.

Meanwhile the consultant at St Peter's (I learned from the notes in 2002) should have diagnosed me with IC at the latest by 25/4/78.

Of course I have no proof that the diagnosis was DELIBERATELY lost but all evidence points that way. If it was not then it was just bloody incompetence, either way in their rush to label my disease 'psychological' or to cover up negligence (which is more likely) the diagnosis was 'LOST' until April 2000. TWENTY TWO YEARS LATER.

The treatment at that time for IC was primitive. Urethral stretching every three months. In fact, one consultant around this time did say that my bladder was inflamed and shrunken and the only way it could be treated was to do urethral stretching every three months which would help the symptoms but only temporarily.

It is my belief that the NHS KNEW that mistakes had been made and would not admit them or do anything about putting them right.

It was easier to LIE.

The NHS had offered to treat the disease, but they still would not admit it actually existed, and were ready to go on lying to protect consultants.

Interlude

So I was now already in the end stage of a disease that did not officially exist. I was taking antibiotics on repeat prescription and had been since 1977 – for an infection that did not officially exist.

I had been repeatedly lied to. Repeatedly told I was a 'head case'.

Things could not get any worse.

No?

Still determined to find out the truth and to get well – and with a GP who would not do anything to get me out of his surgery because of course there was nothing wrong with me! I ended up at The Royal Free Hampstead.

Here again I asked for a cystectomy – here again it was refused.

I was by now also taking antidepressants to keep me sane. I had given up trying to fight the gloom, T and her daft notion I was 'sick', the pain, the illness and the sleepless nights and had decided that if the only way life was bearable was from a pill bottle then so be it. Me who hated any form of medication that acted on the brain. Besides it was risky.

Take antidepressants gives another reason to be labelled a nutter.

I explained to my GP why I needed the antidepressants.

"What do you expect, you have a very depressing disease," was his reply. So my disease actually EXISTED. It had been acknowledged and not only acknowledged but acknowledged as depressing. It was one of the very few sensible things I have ever heard from the NHS.

I went into the chapel at the Royal Free to pray. Not that I had much faith in God left but I had prayed now for six years each time I went into hospital to die under the anaesthetic (and was always disappointed to wake up.)

This time I also prayed that they would find out how ill I was and remove my bladder.

On coming around from the anaesthetic alive and not too happy I was again told I had trigonitis, (inflammation caused by infection) a small inflamed bladder – and at least it was confirmed again my disease was real.

I asked again for a cystectomy – again was refused.

I went back to the chapel before leaving. I did not pray I just sat there and thought, so what now, where to now, why? I closed my eyes for a moment and on opening them I looked at the altar. There was no altar. Where the altar had been was an operating table, the lights above the altar were theatre lights. I closed my eyes again thinking I had now gone completely mad, and when I opened them there in front of me was the altar again. Standing on it was a man in a white coat, he was holding up in his hands a bloody dripping object and he was smiling.

Had I known it would be another 22 years in the future when this operation was to finally be done I would not have been smiling!

So many times I have seen 'pictures' of the future like

this while asleep or awake but not usually so clearly.

So now in 1979 circumstances were slowly worsening. I had had enough of living with T in Wembley. Finding accommodation in London was impossible. I was stuck in a no win situation. Looking back there was NO way out.

It had to be lived through, gone through. So I took each day, worked through the pain, kept my mouth shut. Learned not to show emotion. Waited to die, prayed to die. Inside I was already dead. The only thing keeping me going was hope and the belief that I was going to be well one day, so perhaps it is better looking back that I did not know just how ill I was. Also of course there was B who I still saw, in this sea of madness. Healing did nothing for me but to go and talk to someone who believed I was ill, someone who understood pain and illness.

One day a reading with M, a friend of B's who was a psychic, something came up – "It is important that you do not use aluminium in any form. Do not use aluminium kettles, saucepans etc, you could be poisoned by aluminium. Maybe this is the cause of your disease."

Now it sounded strange but M was so accurate on so many other things so on returning home I threw out all my aluminium saucepans believing that now I might have a chance to get well. I knew only enough about aluminium poisoning to know it affected the brain so at least I decided I will never get brain poisoning.

How near the truth. The wrong metal!

Meanwhile life with T was getting worse – if that was possible.

Now due to being ill and in pain, no sleep at nights due to pain etc, no energy due to no sleep, I kept falling asleep during the day. This could happen at any time, one minute wide awake, next asleep.

"Wake up," she would scream at me again and again.

I hadn't even felt tired, I thought it was strange to fall asleep in the middle of the day, but with my health in the mess it was in I did not question it too much.

"It's all psychological, you are sick, you sleep to get away from life," she snapped at me. Now much as I would have liked then to 'get away from life' I knew deep down that the cause was physical, but trying to explain it was not possible with her. I was later to find out that this sleeping was due to my body being poisoned by mercury!

Pain, illness, infection etc were all 'in my head.' I needed a psychiatrist according to her.

I spent as much time as I could away from the house. I wanted to spend my weekends in bed, just putting up with the pain. I MADE myself go out. I MADE myself get away from the house. Just to be away from her. When she made friends with the couple next door I hoped that now she would spend more time with them and let me off the hook. She did – and told them I was 'sick'.

Now I needed someone to talk to. T's friend next door and I became friends. T took over and it wasn't safe. A had been having problems with her husband and was not eating properly, T then decided she was sick. I could see the same emerging pattern, and began at last to realise that T was dangerous.

The sleeping continued.

I stayed sane with repeated trips to Brighton, trying to keep out of her way, but wherever I went, work, out or asleep her voice kept repeating to me – you are sick. I had to get out of that house or I would go as daft as she thought I was.

In the end I said I had had enough. A row followed, "After all I have done for you etc etc."

"If you leave leave now."

I stayed, it was there or the street.

Knowing what I know now I should have taken my chances with the street.

In May 1980 they both decided they were going to sell the house and move to Spain. This was it, I would HAVE to get out. Nothing could be as bad. Back to the way it had been in early 1976. However small the room, it would be ON MY OWN. I could be myself.

Over the last year I had attended 63 appointments, hospitals/doctors/alternative/complementary   therapist all hidden from T. It was easier to lie. Some helped a little (the alternative ones) but of course the disease was already in the end stage. No alternative/complementary therapy (with the exception of healing) could have done any good. I did not know that then – I just lived on hope.

Meanwhile knowing the house was to be sold, I said I was saving for a flat. This was not true. I could never have afforded a flat. I did not want a flat I wanted my health.

This pleased everyone who now started treating me like a normal human being. At last you are spending your money on something sensible instead of silly things (silly things being my health).

For a little while I kept up the pretence.

So onto August 1980 – The Homeopathic Hospital London.

Here again another cystoscopy – my fifth.

Here the truth (briefly).

My whole urinary tract from the kidneys down was inflamed, infected and scarred. My bladder was grossly shrunken, dilation was tried – it did not work, just caused bleeding. The consultant admitted mistakes had been made (the only consultant to EVER do so), said it was a tragic situation in a young girl. He apologised – again the only consultant to ever do so.

"Will I die?" I asked.

"Yes."

"How long have I got?"

"At the most 2 years."

I was still in my twenties I had just been told again I had only two years to live. The two years to follow would be hell but there would be an end to it. Thank God. Yes, two years of intolerable pain, illness, but an END to it.

I phoned T and told her everything EXCEPT that it was to kill me. Her reply, even for HER shocked me.

"Well you will have to learn to live with it and you had better be smiling when I come and see you."

At that moment I hated her.

How could anyone be so indifferent, so callous?

So I told her not to bother coming. This from me apparently shocked her.

Her daughter told me, "Mum can't forgive you for what you said."

"Tell her I will never forgive her for what she said."

And I never have although I have tried, have made every excuse. It was the sickest remark I have ever heard. I swore I would never go near another hospital again I would rather just let nature take its course. But the course was painful and unbearable so in March 1981 I found myself back at St Peter's (third time).

From the notes (2002) the senior registrar refers to my appointment with the psychiatrist in November 1974, still ignoring the fact he said I was normal, wasting his time and sent me to a consultant urologist at UCH (funny how this piece of information KEEPS turning up and never gets lost like every other! Decides much of it is 'psychological' writes that before considering a urinary diversion – a standard treatment for INTERSTITIAL CYSTITIS, we must get a urodynamic test done. A test which would have been totally useless and invasive. So again proof that the NHS KNEW I had IC. So why LIE and say my disease is 'all in my head.'?

To add insult to injury, this fool tried to fob me off with valium.

Big mistake – I now put the valium to good use. Without it I could not have tried to end my life. Now a lot of rubbish is written about suicide – usually by those who know nothing about it.

1. It is NOT a cry for help/attention etc. – certainly in MY case it was a serious attempt to end my life – or at least speed up the ending I was NOT waiting another 18 months, I was going now.
2. It's easy – it's not even then when I really wanted to die every instinct cries out against it, which is why I took the valium to calm me down enough to do it.
3. If it does NOT work at least people do something about the cause, in this case sort out my health – rubbish they just think you are weird.

While I was being stitched up the nursing sister asked me why I did it.

I told her and she openly laughed in my face. "Women don't kill themselves just because they have cystitis."

"Ever had it?" I asked her.

In fact the suicide rate is very high 12% of women with IC either seriously contemplate suicide or actually kill themselves.

"Now we have to contact someone," she said. "In case

you try to do it again." Rubbish the last thing you want to do is try it again!

I had a choice, T or the police. Now I think I should have taken my chance with the police. Then I chose T because she had less chance legally of having me sectioned. Wrong choice again.

I arrived home in a taxi. T treated me as if I was some kind of sick animal. Told everyone – who looked at me as if I was some kind of alien species. Now you MUST have psychiatric treatment – must I hell.

That was on the Friday, well in those days the patient HAD to see their GP although not a criminal offence, people were often treated that way.

My GP for once went into a sensible mood, and agreed that there was no point in my seeing a psychiatrist when it was my BODY that was sick.

It was the most sensible thing I have ever heard him say!

On the Monday (I had cut my wrists on the Friday) I got ready for work. "You are going to work?" says T.

"Well of course I am going to bloody work, what do you expect me to do stay home and discuss which shrink I see?"

From then for nearly a year things deteriorated. I did not pretend to even like her. She told everyone she knew I was mental, it was a joke that I had tried to end my life because of my disease (which did not exist anyway). She denied talking about me (even when I heard her). For over a year I wanted to get out, I felt trapped in that house, there was nowhere to go to. I just waited to die. Longed to die.

Finally one day A her friend said to me, "They have sold the house."

I can remember so clearly where I was that day, the moment I learned that I would soon be free. I would HAVE to move. Fate had intervened.

Had I known how long it would be until they actually did move I would not have been so confident. I spent hours when I was too ill to go out just staring at the sign outside my window. I still have the photo of it.

It kept me sane.

I was going to get away.

Away to where no one thought I was mad.

Away to just one small room anywhere to end my life – on my own.

I had been there eight years. I was 30. My life was soon to be over. I could not wait. I did not fear death, only dying, slowly, in pain, ill, I did not know or care if there was a life after death. I only wanted oblivion.

Chapter 5

Still on the carrots

May 1992-June 1990

Well I found somewhere to live, a bedsitter in a shared house again, within walking distance from work. The top floor was lived in by a couple and I had the end room. Completely separate. This was as good as any other place to die. A shed would have done, I did not care, I was away from T, that was all that mattered.

I was free, I was allowed to cry, allowed to grieve, allowed to admit I was in pain. Allowed to admit I was ill. I could go to a doctor, hospital, clinic etc whenever I wished. There was no one to tell me that I was mental, because I would not accept the "minor" disease that had ruined my life. There was no-one there to call me sick, or tell anyone else I was sick. Despite being so ill I still carried on working. I am not sure why.

It was doing me no good but deep down I knew either I must die, or I must get well, there was no in between.

I had no intention of going on day after day, year after year suffering in silence, because officially there was nothing wrong with me.

To my annoyance I always woke up the next day – when I was able to sleep from the pain, or not up all night with the 'imaginary' infection.

One thing I was sure of, IF I ever recovered enough to contemplate having a relationship I was not going to have children.

The very thought of taking the risk of having any daughter of mine inherit my disease was abhorrent. So I decided to have myself sterilised.

Now even with my medical history in the 1980s getting sterilised when you are a single childless woman was difficult. Even if you were very ill!

I had tried two years before. The first time the gynecologist I asked had told me, "No – there is no guarantee that the disease will be passed on."

My reply that we were talking about a child who could be born with a horrible disease, not a bloody washing machine that can be sent back for a refund if found to be defective, did not go down very well.

I then contacted Marie Stopes clinic who after counselling, (then compulsory) agreed to operate as long as I had someone with me to take me home afterwards because of the anaesthetic.

I asked B and she said to book the appointment for the operation and she would accompany me. So I did then, "I can't come up to London now the weather is too cold."

I waited another year and a half booked the appointment again and was told, "Not now, the weather is too hot!" (B's excuses were never very original.)

So this was the THIRD time I tried. After explaining the situation to Marie Stopes they agreed that I could come unaccompanied providing I stayed in a nearby hotel for the night. So it was booked (third time lucky) of course I told no-one – NOTHING was going to stop this operation.

For the first time in my life I was treated like a normal

human being by the medical profession, my first taste of a private clinic.

The operation was due to be done at 9.30 but the anesthetist was late. Every twenty minutes a nurse came in, reassured me he was on his way, asked if I needed anything and apologised for keeping me waiting.

I felt as if I had already had the anaesthetic – this just was not reality! During that 2 hour wait every irrational thought went through my mind. That my family had somehow found out and would stop the operation. That something would go wrong at the last minute.

Finally he arrived. At 11.30 on 28 July 1982, the needle went into my hand, it was one of the three happiest moments of my life.

Now I could never pass on this crippling disease to ruin another life.

My GP for some strange reason told me he was putting on my sick note to work that I had had a bladder operation (I never found out why he did this or cared). He could have put on the notes I had had a bloody sex change (much less common then!) for all I cared.

The notes I found in 2002 when I filed the medical negligence claim do record the operation, so officially it existed.

Research now shows that the disease is almost guaranteed to be passed on. Daughters born to mothers with IC are not only inheriting the disease but are developing it at an earlier age than when their mothers began to have symptoms.

In all the case histories I have done a close female relative either has IC symptoms or a history of bacterial cystitis, the chance of inheriting is at least 17%, and daughters can inherit from fathers who have IC.

Also the fact that I was sterilised was proof that the disease existed – no-one even then would sterilise a young woman, unmarried and childless without a good reason and certainly not one who was supposed to be mental!

I was still seeing A occasionally but never talked to her about anything important. How could I? T had convinced her I was mental. How could I have said to her (even if she was supposed to be a friend) "I am very ill, in intolerable pain, and I just can't cope anymore."

I know what she would have replied, I have heard it all before.

"Aren't you lucky you don't have cancer?"

"You are not going to die so what is the problem?" I never told anyone of my supposed approaching death. "Why don't you get yourself a boyfriend?"

"Why don't you go out and meet people?"

"If doctors say it is all in the mind, it must be."

By now anyone else would have given up work – not me.

Yes maybe it was what I should have done, it would at least have drawn attention to the fact I was so ill and someone MAY have intervened.

I often look back and think is this where it all went completely wrong, was it MY fault I carried on instead of giving in?

Should I just have quietly lay down and just faded out?

If I had screamed help me I am in pain would anyone have listened?

Or would they have decided I was mad and sent for the nearest psychiatrist?

If the NHS HAD discovered I was in the end stages of IC would they have operated? And if yes would they have bodged the operation?

Probably, my work has brought me in touch with some

ladies who have had poor or botched operations and one stoma nurse has admitted it goes on.

I needed the money for private Complementary/Alternative treatment.

So I carried on working. The jury is still out on whether this was the right thing to do.

For the last eight years I had had symptoms of a prolapsed womb, along with everything else.

"You can't have prolapse you have not had any children," I was told. Rubbish a virgin nun can have one. Each month for eight years ALL my symptoms improved dramatically when I had a period it had got to the point where I welcomed my period so much as for two whole days in a month I felt so much better. Coincidence said every GP/consultant.

So I took myself off to a private Complementary clinic in Surrey and saw a gynecologist who confirmed my womb was in the wrong position and also pointed out this was what may be causing the urinary disease.

Rubbish said doctors who refused to refer me for operation.

So he inserted a pessary ring, or tried to.

The ring would NOT stay in place. He tried three, each one larger than the other. Difficult to insert, the last one almost impossible.

The only way I could stand having the damn thing inserted was to get drunk first so I was relaxed enough for him to do it.

I have no idea what the receptionist thought when I came in half cut drinking what was obviously not water, and smelling of drink but he did put the final one in, and he advised me to have surgery.

So back to my GP.

I went back to Wembley Hospital.

After the usual old crap 'you saw a psychiatrist back in the year dot you must be a nutter' conversation. The doctor, female this time agreed to examine me.

Now I had just told her I had had a dirty great pessary ring inserted to hold off the womb.

"What is this?" she asked when her probing fingers found the ring.

I refrained with great difficulty in saying, "Well it's a wedding ring but we got married in secret so I keep it up my **** what do you think it is you stupid bitch?"

And again repeated what I had just told her.

She washed her hands and her tea arrived.

Now I can deal with the male idiots of the medical profession but not the females. I expect them to at least listen and remain remotely focused so when she then started pouring out her tea then drinking it and ignoring me I had had enough.

"Are you going to operate? I asked her.

She ignored me.

"I asked you a question, will you please answer me, and put that bloody tea down a moment."

She stared at me open mouthed.

"Are you going to operate?"

"Mr --- will operate if you pay him."

"He WILL operate or I will report you and the remark you have just made." He operated!

In October of that year I ended up at St Bart's London.

According to my notes (2002) I had 'irritable bladder' which means precisely nothing! And he tried to give me valium – which of course I refused – so he told me I was mental. Someone around this time suggested counselling – not because they thought I needed it, but because a counsellor may be able to put in writing that my disease was physical and make things move. I had obviously not learned enough from the shrink at Wembley who was going to put it in writing that I was normal. Luckily I never actually got as far as seeing this weirdo the phone conversation was enough.

"Do you masturbate?" said this female voice.

My first thought was that I had phoned the wrong number and got the local sex shop courtesy of BT.

"I think I have the wrong number," I managed to stammer out. "I have cystitis and am trying to sort things out as I have been wrongly told it is due to mental problems."

"Yes that's right, cystitis is caused by masturbation," she replied.

"Are you some sort of sick pervert?" I shouted before slamming down the phone.

I have no idea looking back why I never reported this woman.

Probably because I did not think anyone would believe me.

Sadly this is NOT an isolated incident. The world of psychiatrists and counsellors attracts more weirdos than any other profession – I was just unlucky I was told many years later. I consider myself lucky. Lucky never to have met her!

Finally in desperation I went back to the Aston, a private clinic I had found in New Malden where they practised complementary medicine and saw a hypnotherapist.

"I have heard that any disease can be cured/improved with hypnotherapy," I said.

"Yes it can but only if the disease or part of it is in any way psychological/psychosomatic and yours is NOT."

November 1982 – again referral from work I ended up at the Samaritan hospital for women in London.

Now I assumed that being a women's hospital the consultant would be a woman, I was very disappointed to find it was a man and angry when he told me wrongly that my disease was mental. By now I was not only getting angry that I kept being labelled mental, I was getting very suspicious. I sounded normal, acted normal was normally intelligent, how could doctors who had never met me been so quick to label me mental? Something wasn't right and it could not JUST have been the fact that I saw Dr B at Wembley and things had been turned round. Something was WRONG.

1st December 1982

Well now I had the appointment to see the consultant at Wembley to see if he would operate. I was ready for him – ultimatum – either he operated or I reported what had been said in September. He agreed to operate, to be honest I had gone in prepared for a fight. So I went to admission to book a date.

"It will be at least 9 months." said the receptionist.

"It won't," was my reply, "I have waited eight years already."

"Well it's not urgent," she said.

"It's urgent to me, this disease has ruined my life it's urgent."

"OK then, can you come in at a moment's notice?" she asked.

"I'll come in now if you like," I replied.

To her credit she put me on the cancellation list. I came in for the operation two weeks later.

I was due to arrive at 9.00 I arrived at 8.15.

"You will have your operation as you are the first one here," I was told. There are five women booked into your bed!

And they say there is a crisis in the NHS NOW!

So the operation was finally done. EIGHT YEARS ON.

For two years there was a slight improvement in my symptoms, then the womb moved again. NHS refused to sew it back as again I was imagining it. It was to be another TEN years until it was removed completely and things began to improve. I had learned one thing this year I did not know before.

Stand your ground.

Shout.

Argue.

Complain.

The wheel that squeaks loudest gets the oil!

In January 1983 there was a breakthrough.

I consulted Dr Mount (a Naturopath) in London.

He put me on a diet of just salad, fruit and vegetables and in three days all the secondary infections cleared and my cystitis improved 100%. I felt on top of the world, stopped the antibiotics for two weeks.

Then came a kidney infection. Now of course it was obvious that the infection was a healing crisis, my body was beginning to heal. I did not know this nor could I continue for too long on only fruit and vegetables and salad, BUT, I had learned the connection between food and illness.

My next step was to go to the Burgh Heath Clinic in Banstead, Surrey run by John Mansfield the famous allergist. Then the knowledge that food allergy caused illness was in its infancy and such people were seen as quacks and their patients were seen as deluded.

"Is it near the looney bin?" my colleagues at work would ask me. (Banstead hospital was still open then.)

"Still on the carrots," my landlord would laugh at me, "why do you go to these quacks?"

Well the 'quack' discovered something – when I was injected with a weak dose of rice I immediately developed the symptoms of a severe kidney infection. Was it ALL allergy, was it really that simple?

Is that why I had been told no infection could be found? But if so why was I continually on antibiotics for an infection that did not exist?

Had the NHS been truthful with me instead of lying through their teeth things may have been different.

John Mansfield pointed out that the overuse of antibiotics had caused Candida infection and other secondary infections, "Whoever has given you long term antibiotic treatment should be struck off. These have upset your immune system and the whole of your body. You MUST stop taking antibiotics, they are doing you no good whatsoever." So I tried – the infection returned so severely I had to go back.

The pain was horrendous, my whole body was shaking and I felt so ill. So I stayed on the antibiotics, at least they were knocking the edge off the symptoms.

So to June 1983 one of the lowest periods of my life.

I was in a catch-22. Could not stop the antibiotics, very ill, looking back I realise how ill.

I found that the only thing that helped the pain was alcohol – one drink knocked the edge off it two made it worse.

So in the evenings or at night when I had given up all

chance of sleep (most nights) I would have a drink.

No there was no danger of my ending up with a drink problem I had the sense to restrict it and see alcohol as a medicine/pain killer and not a way of life, and as my kidneys were supposed to be failing anyway – that was taking its time! I did not really care.

Then I lived near a railway line and each night I wished I had the guts to go down the embankment and lay my head on the line and wait for a train.

I did not have the guts to do it though. Just the common sense not to tell anyone. The suicide rate in IC patients may be understandably very high but of course I was not ill I was not in pain officially, it was 'all in my head', besides people who chose to die rather than suffer are crazy, 'need help' was the polite phrase. Nothing has changed much!

So I spent most nights then praying to find the guts – I never did.

Finally I went to my GP and asked for antidepressants again – I hated to do this but if I had to spend the rest of what was left of my life on pills to give me just a little taste of happiness then so be it. Hopefully it would not be for long and nature would take its course.

I hate to ask for these things I said, "Well what do you expect it is a very depressing illness," was the reply, again!

I wrote to P who by now was a qualified homeopath to ask if she could help me.

All through the rest of the summer of 1983 I laid on the grass in Golders Hill Park, praying that things would change, praying for the operation that would end my suffering or praying to die.

Nothing much had really changed since I left T.

People still thought I was crazy/still thought I was

putting it on or imagining illness/still thought I was making a fuss over nothing.

Going to work each day, swallowing antidepressants and waiting patiently for the end.

Then P replied to my letter – and things changed.

Chapter 6

HOPE

(Oct 1983-Sept 1986)

"Forget everything you have been told, your disease is physical, you are going to get well."

I remember that first visit so well. Sitting in that bright room in Bishopstone with P feeling for the first time that things were going to change, that my body would heal and at last I would have a life and a future.

That Autumn of 1983 when I threw away the antidepressants that I had decided to spend the rest of my life on rather than take any more pain. Someone cared, someone believed I was physically ill, someone believed I would get well, someone was on my side.

On my third visit we took her dog for a walk over to the local church in Bishopstone. P told me how lovely the churchyard looked in Spring when the daffodils were out. For a moment my mind crossed time, the churchyard was full of daffodils and I was told then I would be happy.

It was the first of many walks in 1983/1984 walks that did me more good than any medicine or treatment. There was a world outside Wembley, one day I would walk in it free of pain and illness. I believed it would last.

I believed I would soon be well. P was a healer and homeopath and now a friend. One who understood, someone who did not think I was crazy/attention seeking. From her I learned that it was OK to feel, OK to cry, OK to feel depressed, OK to admit that life could be shit, and OK to hope.

From her I learned that the greatest gift that you can ever give when someone is so ill is the gift of HOPE.

That summer of 1984 was one of the happiest in my life. I was still in a lot of pain, still very ill but I was allowed to admit it existed. I did not have to hide it any more.

I could admit I was very depressed and had every right to be.

On the Saturday mornings when I travelled down to Sussex I dreamed of the future, free of pain, free of illness, free to have a life. Then I would move to Sussex – I loved the area, the country the sea.

What I did not know then was that I was in the end stage of my disease, although P did tell me a few months later that my body would soon have packed up, things could not have gone on much longer.

I was not naive enough to think I would get well overnight but through – maybe this time next year I will be a little better.

For Christmas 1984 she gave me a diary and I would mark in it each day I did not need antibiotics.

"I walked over to the church yesterday, I thought of you."

"You can phone me anytime, I will always listen."

But the change did not come all at once.

"I see you each month, a little progress each time."

She did not see the times when I went down the beach after seeing her and cried for my pain, for my lost future, for the way T had treated me. For my lost life, and for the times I asked WHY? What had I done. "Why me?"

And why of all the horrible disease to get – this one?

"One day you will have a flat, you will be well, you will be happy, you will get married, you will travel."

It took sixteen years to get well and get the flat, one day I may travel but no, I will never marry.

"There will come a day when you do not have to come here anymore, you will say goodbye you will forget."

I have never forgotten.

January 1990

I did try to forget, did try to let go, but this morning I travelled down to Seaford Head again, walked where we walked, heard your voice again and for a moment I had hope.

I was now in the end stages of IC and did not have a clue. Looking back thank God I did not know, there was nothing P could have done.

I needed major surgery – sometimes it is better not to know. Not knowing saved my life.

Spring 1984

I have been off antibiotics a whole week. I told P and I am feeling much better.

I don't go down to the beach and cry anymore, I don't live from day to day, I don't want to die, I am standing in the churchyard surrounded by daffodils and I feel happy.

I went back to the clinic in Banstead. Tests showed the secondary symptoms were partly due to food allergy, the cause of the kidney infection and cystitis are still a mystery.

"Come in, you are one of the family now."

We talked about a picnic, we took photos, I laughed, "I want you to think of me as a friend."

Happy summer days in her garden, still very ill physically. P explained something to me that day and it is so true.

It is all right to be ill for a short time, people care then they get bored, they don't bother anymore, disease frightens them.

September 1984

P had given me a book "The Grape Cure" in February. Of course I had halfheartedly read it but was not too interested. How could grapes cure what antibiotics could not?

I was then on eight antibiotics a day. (I should have been taking four!)

I had a severe kidney infection and could not care less if I lived or died.

I booked a week's holiday off work and started the grape diet on 1st September 1984. By the evening of that day I was feeling 100% better.

By the evening of the next day the infection had completely gone. Grapes had done in two days what antibiotics had failed to do. For five days I continued on this diet until driven by intense hunger I stopped. For two weeks I did not need antibiotics and I felt so well.

In 1985 I circled in my diary each day I could cope without antibiotics. 37 circles – five weeks free.

I have now been off antibiotics 4 months I told P.

What I had dreamed about for so long had happened. I was not going to spend the rest of my life on antibiotics and painkillers – but of course it could not last. In Sept 1985 the infection came back with a vengeance.

Meanwhile while all this was happening in the Summer of 1984 my brother was married.

My great aunt V, the only relative in my family I was still

in touch with and the only one who believed I was actually very ill, and not 'imagining' my disease, and the only one who ever gave me any support phoned me and told me.

"I am not going," I said to P. "I haven't seen my family for years, have no wish to, especially my mother and I feel too bloody ill."

"You will regret it if you do not," said P. So I went, and regretted it!

I travelled down from Wembley to Devon on a train overnight. I do not remember too much about the journey except for feeling permanently sick, being doubled up with pain, very ill and if it had not been for the fact that it was an overnight train I would have got off, crossed the platform and gone straight home.

I had taken twice the amount of painkillers and antibiotics than I usually had to knock the edge off the pain. (It was 2000 before I learned that at that stage I should have been on morphine for the pain – no one ever offered me morphine, or anything much else because of course the pain did not officially exist!)

I had also promised my great aunt I would go, and he was my brother, it was not his fault he had been the favourite, nor was he responsible for the abuse I received.

I had already missed two family funerals, which of course had caused rows as my disease did not officially exist so of course I was lying when I said I was too ill to travel. Anyone with IC knows what a nightmare travelling can be, and also knows how ignorant others can be in ignoring how difficult it is.

My mother was distantly polite, as was I, which was just how I wanted it. I was in no mood for pretending we actually liked each other.

At the reception, which by now with the extra

antibiotics and painkillers I was just aware of my mother's voice talking to her daughter in law's relatives.

"Janet does not come to see us, we do not know what it is all about."

I looked up and saw her face, the same sick sweet evil smile.

I never saw her after that day, and never had any contact with her again. That sick smile and the mistake I made in believing she might have changed haunted me until I heard she was dead in 1997.

In July 1985 P introduced me to R. An acupuncturist. Now there were two kind people taking an interest, treating me, helping me, believing in me. Again there was nothing R could have done that would have done any good, the disease was in its last stage but I did not know that then.

Although I was not feeling any better I still believed I would be well. Had I not been off antibiotics for nearly nine months?

Although I was now back on them permanently I still hoped, still dreamed.

Feeling ready to die I crawled down to Sussex again and asked R for healing.

He put his hands on my back and I felt as if I had an electric fire near me. I crawled home again into bed and slept. Next morning when I woke up the pain had gone and I did not feel ill. This lasted two weeks. There was the proof I was curable.

February 1986

I was feeling very low. I had been off work two weeks with a serious kidney infection (for some reason I have

72

never worked out it was always admitted that the kidney infections existed but not cystitis) and was seriously thinking of giving up work. Working while I was so ill and in so much pain was impossible, especially when you are not allowed to admit you are ill or in pain because there is nothing really wrong with you is there it's 'all in the mind' or nothing much.

I wanted to die, then the doorbell rang. It was H from work my friends mother with flowers and a card from her daughter and a work colleague. I carried on working! Then came the day I could take no more. I had been travelling to work with H for 3 months now. I tried all through the journey to try to tell her then it all came pouring out and I could not stop crying – and she listened – did not tell me to shut up she just listened.

"All I can do is sympathize."

ALL?

For years I had longed and hoped for someone to do just that, and apart from P and B no one had cared and all she could do was sympathize!

She said she would come with me to see a specialist I MUST see one.

I will never forget the words she said to me when we arrived at work, "This may sound funny love, do you have faith?"

"Yes."

"You are half way there love."

Later on that day she asked me how I was feeling and on the journey home she said, "You poured out your heart to me this morning, you must not bottle things up it is the worst thing you can do. You can talk to me anytime I will always listen." And she always did. Turned off the radio and listened, and H never said or thought I was crazy, never told me I needed counselling or any other rubbish, she believed I was physically ill. And so it continued for over 18 months – someone else cared.

But I never asked her to come with me to a specialist or the doctors. I was afraid she would then believe I was incurably ill, would believe my disease was 'imaginary'.

I was afraid of breaking the spell that was giving me hope and keeping me alive, and sane. The dream of a tomorrow, the dream of a future. The dream of a life without pain or illness. And still twenty-six years later I still remember the sun rising over the memorial outside Buckingham Palace, the flowers on the embankment and a woman who gave the hope and strength to carry on.

When everyone else thought I was an incurable crazy.

April 1986

I had found the specialist who had told me six years ago at the London Homeopathic that I was incurably ill. He had had the guts to be truthful then, perhaps he could help me again.

Strangely the only thing that seemed to concern him at first were the scars on my wrists. Now of course almost every doctor I see looks first at the scars on my wrists, and usually no further, which is another reason I avoid doctors.

He arranged for another IVP which showed a refluxing ureter. He told me that this was not important why did I believe this – well he had been honest before so I trusted him. Years later I was to learn that refluxing ureter WAS very important although not in the end the cause but how had it been missed before, (if it HAD been missed) not just ignored, why had no one questioned it?

May 1986

"Are you still going to Sussex?" H asked.

"Am I really going to get well?" I asked P.

"Yes, because you want to and that is half the battle."

"Have you ever tried hormone treatment?" the private female doctor asked me.

"No, I have been asking for over ten years if hormones could be part of the problem but no one has taken a blind bit of notice."

So she tried hormones but it did not make any difference – but at least she tried, she also knew a private urologist and sent me to him.

"Is there any sign of infection?" was the first stupid question he asked me. I refrained from asking him why the hell he thought I had been taking antibiotics continually for so many years if there was not, with great difficulty.

I want PROOF he shouted slamming his fist hard on the desk (I want a doctor not a tantruming child) I thought.

He then went onto tell me I was incurably ill (without examining me) and suggested the usual fob off tests.

I need something more positive I replied.

He said I was wasting his time and told me to go. I did not need telling! Then he told his receptionist there was no charge. Did he really expect me to PAY for that charade!

August 1986

Clementine Churchill was an expensive private hospital in Harrow. Fantastic reputation I was told. My GP managed to mess the whole thing up by sending me to a urologist with details only of the gynecological history but at least he did not write and say I was crazy, which was a bonus then!

Without even an examination I was told I had an incurable bladder disease.

My GP then wrote in a letter that I had been under ten NHS hospitals that had failed to diagnose my chronic urinary infection (so it exists then).

I am on continuous antibiotic therapy to maintain life, stated that there was no gynecological cause for my deteriorating urinary symptoms and concluded, that I should see a psychiatrist!

Luckily I did not learn of this bizarre letter until May 2002 via my solicitor and a barrister! Mentally I went back six years. The only difference now was that I could confide in someone.

L (my friend) said to me, "You have more guts than everyone in this office put together."

It was comforting yes but guts – I would rather have been a first class coward and have my health.

Two weeks later I tried St Stephen's Hospital London. It is supposed to be very good I was told. Well it is – if you had AIDS. AIDS was the trendy thing then, we were all supposed to be going to die of it, there was an epidemic.

Well I had high hopes that day – gynecological symptoms meant I could hardly walk had profuse discharge, etc.

Doctor twat examined me – "It's all very healthy down there," he said.

P phoned to cancel our appointment that weekend. "I will tell you why when I see you again," she said. I had already guessed. We were going to part. I was going to lose the help, support and healing that had kept me going and given me hope and a reason to live for three years. So we said goodbye, I had no idea then that I would not see her for a few years, or how she would change.

The last time I would sit in that bungalow and be given hope, P gave me my notes and I read them on the train. I did not remember so much the things that were written of the pain, the nightmares, the illness but I did remember for many years after:

- Being told to think of her as a friend.
- Being told I was loved.
- Being told I was thought of.
- Being allowed to cry and to feel.
- Being allowed to admit I was ill.
- Being told I had guts.

Well P would not have thought I had guts if she had seen me a few weeks later. I don't remember how it began or if anything triggered it, I only know I went into madness, and I have never been so afraid in my life and never so glad that I lived alone.

The worst period covered only three days but it was two weeks before I could say I was normal again.

I found myself lying on my bed and heard a sound like an animal in pain, a wailing, sound and it was some time before I became conscious that the sound was coming from me.

It seemed to be coming from a long way off. Then this crying erupted from me, not the normal crying of complete despair but from deep within as though I was spewing up the past seventeen years, all at once.

Each doctor, each hospital visit, each negative response, seventeen years of pain, illness frustration was fighting to get into my mind at once.

Every fear, the abuse, the memories trying to get out all at once.

After two days I vaguely remembered it was Monday and I should have been at work.

H rang the doorbell and I told her through the letterbox I was too ill to go to work. (Of course I did not say why!) I wanted to call her back, ask her to help me but even through the lunacy I knew what would happen if I did. Doctors, a looney bin while my real disease continued unchecked. I tried alcohol, antidepressants, nothing stopped it, nothing had any effect on it.

For three days this went on with a few periods of lucidity, during which I tried without success to contact P and R. The periods of lucidity began to get longer but still the crying would erupt.

I was afraid of going back to work, going out, afraid of everything. Somehow I managed to crawl back to work. A medical certificate would have meant questions, probably shrinks etc.

One thing I had learned was to hide my feelings, act normal, control my crying until I was alone.

Back at work I booked a week's holiday to begin the following week. Somehow I managed to carry on working, give the appearance of being normal, holding my feelings inside. No one knew.

When I returned home I would allow the crying and wailing to erupt. Knowing it was safe. No one to see or hear, no one to say I was crazy. I had come through madness, I had come through alone and secretly I had survived.

Chapter 7

Shadows

(Sept 1986-June 1990)

L gave me a lift to the station. "It sounds as if all your trouble is caused by your womb," she said, "why don't you have it removed? If you have it removed even if it is NOT the cause of the trouble you will have at least eliminated it."

"Have you ever tried to get a hysterectomy on the NHS?" I replied.

I had been trying since 1976 to get a hysterectomy, long before I was sterilized even. I KNEW that my womb was part of the cause of the problem. (Later to be proved) I had seen women at work have hysterectomies many of whom did not even want them but had them because a doctor said they should. I had watched for many years women having months off work for hysterectomies, I envied them, hysterectomy was the easiest operation a woman could have then, even if you did not want them! What was wrong with me? Well according to the NHS nothing! I imagined my disease, I was a nut case. When I had asked REPEATEDLY I was either told, "Well you wont be able to have children." (I know that stupid, that is why I was sterilised)

Either that or, "It might make the infection worse."

What infection? Officially it did not exist!

Neither according to the NHS did the sterilization officially exist although I have an X-ray that clearly shows the clips on the tubes!

So I set out to have a hysterectomy come hell or high water.

My GP is useless I told L. "Well why don't you change him?" she replied.

Sounds easy doesn't it, change your GP. Now of course it can be done, back then it was very difficult, besides although I had a GP who was as useless as a chocolate fireguard he did have ONE use. No other GP would have given me the antibiotics I needed to keep me alive on continual prescription for an infection that did not exist. The next three months passed in a blur of antidepressants, and painkillers, and a determination that I WAS going to have a hysterectomy. I had no idea then that I would have to pay for it, lie to beat the system etc. The only consolation during that time was letters from P. "You want to get well and you are doing all you can that is half the battle," she wrote.

When December came round the last thing on my mind was Christmas. The last thing I felt like was celebrating, thank God I was on my own.

I would spend it as I had for all the last years, on my own. Not having to say 'well aren't we all having a wonderful time', while fighting pain and wishing I were dead.

Two days before Christmas on the way to work H said, "Would you like to spend Christmas with us?"

I felt on top of the world and afraid at the same time. Happy because someone was kind and cared about me and afraid I would be ill and in pain.

I had been feeling a bit better this last week and was hoping it would continue. Everything was fine until

Christmas Eve then the pain became worse. By the time H arrived to pick me up I felt like death.

"Don't be afraid, he won't bite you," H said.

I was not afraid of meeting her partner, I was afraid of the pain that was getting worse, becoming unbearable and I would have to hide, as it did not exist. (I should have been taking morphine) H and R went out for a drink with their neighbours and I stayed in longing for a hot water bottle and drugged sleep. I had two days to get through where I must not admit I was in pain or feeling ill, I had to pretend to have a good time, how did I get myself into these situations?

Deep down I wanted the life other people had.

Christmas day and H was very kind, there were just two of us making trifles in the kitchen and talking and me thinking how lucky L was to have such a caring mother.

By the evening people began to arrive and things were getting worse, the painkillers would not even try to hold the pain and everything was a blur of pain and illness. I decided to drink to blot it out, but remained stone cold sober, this Christmas was to be like all the rest – ruined by illness. Finally when I could take no more I followed H out of the room and said I was feeling too ill and in too much pain and did she have any painkillers, and expecting her to be angry.

I can still see her now, standing there in a blue dress saying in an amazed voice, "Why didn't you say?"

Was I hearing right – someone was saying it was OK to be ill and in pain, even at Christmas when everyone was supposed to be happy (or at least pretend they were).

She told me to go to bed and to stay there tomorrow if I did not feel better.

I spent half of Boxing Day in bed and H was very kind and caring.

I began to question had I got it wrong? Should I like

everyone else be allowed to admit I was ill and in pain even if the illness partly involved the lower half of the body. Was this normal?

March 1987

As we drove down Constitution Hill H pointed out the crocuses on the bank.

"Aren't they lovely," she said.

There were crocuses another spring – P showed me. Before I knew it was OK to cry OK to feel. As the seasons changed over that year, from the flowers of spring to the warmth of the summer the beauty of autumn and the cold of winter I was given glimpses of the future, hope of friendship, the belief I would one day be well and have a normal life, the truth would be discovered and I would have health and justice.

I found my health in August 2000 I discovered the truth in May 2002 I am still waiting for justice. Later that month I went up to the church on Harrow Hill. As I sat there again I looked up at the altar, again the figure standing on the altar wearing a white coat, holding in his hands a bloody dripping object.

Later I was awake and there at the end of my bed was my Aunt L and my paternal grandfather, the following conversation took place.

"Janet is going to have an operation."

"It will be an operation to make her well again."

Both these people had been dead for years!

This did not surprise me.

I had often been warned in the past when someone in my family was going to die – and I was never wrong. I had seen events in my own future many times – and not been wrong.

On 9th March four years later I had a hysterectomy and wrongly believed this was the operation. I obtained the name of a private gynecologist in London. Her suggestion that the whole thing could be due to hormones was welcome, she seemed surprised that no one had suggested hormone testing. I wasn't! and the result was she gave me Danazol.

At £80.00 for a month's prescription it was not cheap but I found out that if I stopped taking it then started again I could bring on a period.

As my periods were now practically non existent, down to half a day if I was lucky and this meant one day a month when I would be dramatically free of pain and the urinary symptoms dramatically improved so that one month's living had to be crammed into one day.

Now I could have a period more or less when I wanted one. Fantastic. Probably did not do me any good but did I care. I had given up worrying about the long-term effects of any medication a long time ago. If this shortened or ended my life who cared? I was long past caring. I did not have a life, I had an existence and a very unpleasant one at that.

Nor was I alone.

Now ladies say to me. "I am just waiting for death to release me from this disease." I know just how they feel.

Well it worked for a while but was getting expensive and hard to get the Danazol – especially when officially there is no reason for it. I had realised now where I was going wrong, and obtained the address of a FEMALE consultant. At St. George's Hospital, Tooting.

Just before seeing her I found another truth that had been staring me in the face for years and which I had missed.

I still believed (more fool me) the purpose of a doctor is to help. That they are truthful etc. For the last 8 years my GP had been prescribing antibiotics on a continual prescription basis, so I assume he had a reason for doing so and he knew the infection existed or he would not have prescribed them.

He knew my medical history, he knew how ill I was, he knew I had been so far under seven hospitals. He was also careless enough not to stick the envelope of the letter I was to take to the hospital down properly. Normally I would never have looked – like a fool I trusted him, but something made me open it I read.

'This patient has been investigated at many hospitals they have found nothing wrong with her. She has been advised to seek psychiatric treatment and has refused.'

I made the mistake of thinking this was the ONLY letter of this type that had been written, it was only in 2002 that I discovered it was one of MANY. I wrote my OWN letter How dare this bastard lie and say I was mental! One of many letters I wrote to consultants in the future (mostly ignored) but luckily being a WOMAN she had the intelligence to believe me. She told me I would probably be on antibiotics for the rest of my life and arranged tests, (so much for 'imaginary' illness). I refused one of the tests which I knew was repulsive, degrading, invasive and (as was admitted in 2002 useless) waited for the tests.

I have heard when I am going into hospital I told H. "Good," she said. No, it wasn't good I was terrified.

The day came, H dropped me off at Victoria and I wanted to ask her to drive me into work I wanted it to be a normal day. Why was I putting myself through this?

"Of course it is all connected," said the SEN nurse who booked me in.

"When you have a period the womb lifts off the bladder so you will feel better." She was just an SEN nurse yet she had pointed out what consultants had missed for the last 8 years. Says it all!

As soon as I reached the hospital I felt calm – God knows why. Was this it, was I going to die under the anaesthetic as I had prayed to do for the last six years before each one.

No such luck I woke up again. I tried to push myself back into a world that was blurred and well and pain free.

L came to visit me. There had been a collection at work, the biggest they had ever had she said, people were interested, people wanted to know how I was, people were actually acknowledging I was really ill.

On 10th July 1987 I was told the good news. The scarring had healed, mucosa was healthy, no inflammation, no damage, "I can see no reason why you should stay on antibiotics," she said which frightened me. The infection would come back again.

But I was higher than a kite, my body against all odds was healing then from my GP I found out this was not so.

He mentioned something that had been found which I had not been told. "What causes that?" I asked.

"Untreated infection," was his reply. So I had been lied to AGAIN.

I made up my mind then I would see a solicitor, find out the truth. It took fifteen years before this happened.

"I hope you do not get any worse, you seem to be coping," H told me.

Yes, you see me cope. You don't see me drug myself to sleep, you don't see me drink to ease the pain. You don't see me awake all night crying, then going into work and pretending everything is OK.

If you did you would be like them, 'you need a psychiatrist'.

So I kept quiet, painted my bedsit to try to take my mind off the pain and ended up ill with a stomach upset. I had been breathing in the paint fumes.

Now if paint could cause such a reaction maybe something I was eating, drinking or breathing in could be causing my disease.

Back to John Mansfield Burgh Heath. Four years after my last visit.

Yes a lot of my gynecological symptoms seemed to be connected to food allergy. Candida, and other gyneo symptoms could be produced by injecting certain foods but NOT cystitis or kidney symptoms. And YES food allergy does cause all these, but not in MY case. I started injecting myself with allergy serum so I could eat. An injection every 48 hours. It turned out that the secondary symptoms were aggravating the IC not causing it and no one thought then to test for heavy metals, again the link was missed. But again I had HOPE.

In that autumn of 1987 I truly believed I was going to get well. I had P supporting me, I had hopes, I dreamed of living in Brighton, having my own flat, being well, but hopes and dreams do not cure physical disease and hope died again.

Now slowly and silently another hell was beginning.

In my ignorance I believed that there was a limit to the amount of shit life can chuck at you, that we are each born with a certain amount and when it is over that was it. I wish.

Fate was very soon to prove me wrong. Waiting around the corner was another disease, just as horrible, just as 'incurable'.

Meanwhile, having had more than enough of orthodox medicine and male doctors, I went to the Kent Homeopathic. To see Dr C, a famous homeopathic doctor who has now retired and as I found out later when this happened many people threw a party. She was universally disliked and the word bitch if used to describe her would insult a female dog. I of course was ignorant of all this, to me she was a homeopath and a woman.

Her first comment was I should have gone to the London homeopathic as it was nearer. I told her I had come to Kent because I got nowhere with London. She ignored me and said I should go to London.

Then throughout the consultation she kept muttering 'stress, stress' this was long before it was trendy to be stressed. Then she was called out for something and left the notes she had written on her desk. Bad mistake with me, I was by now used to reading notes (even upside down if necessary). She had written:

'There is nothing wrong with this patient, her disease is all due to stress.'

Which is what she told me when she came back and told me I needed a psychiatrist. What I told her I will not put into print.

April 1988

I went to St Thomas's London and was again offered the invasive and useless test which I declined.

Then in June of that year I had decided I had had enough, was going to get to the truth of what was written on my notes that was preventing me from having treatment that other people took for granted. This was the second time I had tried this.

In 1985 letters had been going back and forth to The Bloomsbury Area Health Authority where I was told Mr C had not passed on the notes that he had thought I was mental (a lie) nor had any other doctor written this (a lie) in all six letters all lying. So I tried the General Medical Council who were of course not interested, then a solicitor who

WRONGLY said that the action would be statute barred.

By now I had other medical problems to contend with. I was beginning to feel numbness in certain areas of my body, first around my mouth on the left side, my face on the left side, sometimes part of my arm or leg would go numb, then back to normal and mostly I did not feel this and only knew it was happening when other people would imitate me. God knows why but that is how people are!

I was a little concerned about the numbness so went to my GP and I asked him if this could be the beginning of MS. He said it was possible and sent me to the National Hospital in London.

Well I walked into that waiting room and nearly walked straight out again (which would have been the best option looking back) the room was full of people, mainly women sitting in wheelchairs, it was like walking into hell. Which I soon found out just about summed it up.

After waiting two hours and forcing myself not to walk out – difficult – I saw a consultant, Dr W. This strange little man had no interest whatsoever in either my neurological symptoms, or my kidney symptoms, he asked me when I last had sex then said, "You don't have MS, what you need is a good F**K."

Now by now I have met many perverts in the NHS (mostly male) but this one shocked, and disgusted me. When I had calmed down – and it took about a week I phoned the hospital and complained about his behaviour and was told they would look into it, then told Dr W no longer works at this hospital – another lie. Eight years later I found out what was really wrong and it had nothing to do with sex or lack of it!

From my notes obtained by my solicitor in 2002, he had written 'I found this patient most difficult, I told her it was most unlikely she had MS. It worries me slightly that she has been on AB continually for 14 years,' and of course he mentioned the scars on my wrist and wrote I was a head case (so what's new) nothing about me needing a good f**k then (perhaps he could not spell it!)

So to a gynecologist in London to try to obtain a hysterectomy (private). Again he confirms I have been on antibiotics for the last 14 years. Still no-one has told me why I am taking antibiotics continually for an infection that does not officially exist!

"Of course your disease is physical any fool can see that." Well of course Y was a woman. She was also a hypnotherapist. I had decided to try hypnosis to try to stop the involuntary movements of the left side of my mouth, also my jaw was moving involuntarily and again I only knew this by other people's negative and hurtful comments and imitating. Anyway I would try anything once and to give Y her due she did try. Of course hypnosis did not work, as it only does so if any part of the disease, however small, has a psychological cause. Mine did not of course so it did not work but gave me hope and kept me sane and with what was to come I needed her support.

In October thinking the jaw problem may be linked to my teeth she sent me to a dentist she knew.

So near the truth now, but again not to be discovered for another four years. We thought it might be a problem with the temporomandibular joint – well it was. Mercury was leaking into it, but no one thought of this.

Meanwhile it was obvious to me that a hysterectomy might help, so I consulted a gynecologist in South London. He said he could not help me as I lived north of the Thames and he only treated patients in South London. Now whether this was true or a fob off did not matter to me. I had two options now, move to South London, or give the impression I lived in South London. Well that was straightforward enough. My Aunt V lived in South London, still the only relative I was in contact with who also believed I was very ill and gave me a little support or who at least listened.

In fact the night before she had said to me, "Let me know if there is anything I can do."

Well I did – I asked her to take in a letter for me and I made the mistake of trusting her with why. "I don't know, I will have to think about it, is it legal?"

I could not believe what I was hearing. This woman knew that I had tried to get this operation for nearly eighteen years all I was asking her to do was take in a letter addressed to me – not to rob a bloody bank! Did I bloody care if it was legal? They could put me in prison for all I cared – in fact I would have had better medical care in prison. This was my life and health, and she had to think about it!

So I saw the gynecologist who said he could see no reason why I could not have a hysterectomy and have it on the NHS. He now believed I was living in South London as I had given the address of an empty property I had found – just by walking the streets and looking for empty properties as you do when you are trying to beat the NHS!

I was also aware that my medical notes with their defamatory statements and lies (the few I knew about then) would not be much help so I decided to ditch the notes. I will not put in print how but it worked temporarily.

So far so good, but of course I had not bargained for the incompetence of the NHS. To avoid correspondence going to an empty house and being lost I said I would collect the admission letters from the surgery I had registered with in Wimbledon. Twice I went back to the surgery and twice they said the letter was not ready, now this was a few weeks later and I was afraid someone had twigged I had given a false address. Then I was told the letter had been sent straight to the hospital. I booked a day off work and went to the hospital to trace the letter and to give my own letter (knowing what might be in a GP's letter I was covering all ways). I asked to see the consultant's secretary and was sent all over the hospital. Finally my patience snapped. I will see him privately just get on with it.

6th March 1990

I saw the consultant, offered to pay, yes the NHS should have sorted out and paid for their own mistakes but if I had gone NHS they would probably have taken the wrong part out and I wanted the job done PROPERLY and NOW. I had waited eighteen bloody years!

He picked up the phone and arranged the operation for 12th March.

Three days. I was over the moon. My firm were not however.

"You have only given two days notice," my boss complained.

Tough I have waited eighteen years for this I am not giving up the chance for them! For the first time since I could remember I went into hospital happy. I did not need to be drugged up to the eyeballs with anything I could get my hands on. I floated in.

In less than 24 hours I would be rid of this useless organ that was contributing to making me so ill. My new life was about to begin.

I was floating until they put in the needle.

Nothing happened – then I was waking up.

The dragging sensation had gone, there was so little pain.

(I was told I would be in horrendous pain following the operation) I was free. No more gynecological infections, no more pressing on my bladder and aggravating and causing cystitis.

"You must rest," I was told. But I did not feel like resting, I wanted to fly. I was at peace for the first time since my disease started, higher than a kite. I was told later they had never seen anyone recover so quickly or look so happy.

I sat in that room for a week recovering, gazing out of the window, dreaming of the life I would now have. There were no complications, (as pessimists told me there would be) no depression (I was told women always suffered from depression following a hysterectomy).

It comes to him who waits – like most things in my life it took a long time a lot of effort and a bit of scheming – but I got there.

Well of course it was not the miracle cure – but as I was to learn many years later the womb contained mercury which had been deposited from the bloodstream. My womb in effect was poisoned.

I learned in 1993 why I should never have had children, and if it were possible to have any, which would have been unlikely, they would have been affected physically, mentally or both.

And apart from one course later that year and about three courses since 2000, I have never taken another antibiotic.

Well life should have improved now, in some ways it had, but nothing is that simple.

The involuntary movement of my mouth and jaw was getting worse.

So was other people's negative attitudes and comments. (It was at least another year before I was to be told I had dystonia.) I returned to work and after the initial. "We were expecting you back two weeks ago." I had only 2 and a half months off work instead of three. I wanted to go back after 2 but my doctor then advised me to take another two weeks. Things for a few weeks were a little better – but some women were a bit strange. They almost resented the fact that I had been off work ill – because officially there was nothing wrong with me was there.

Also I was sick of walking down the street and being laughed at and imitated because of the involuntary movement of my mouth and jaw.

I had had enough of London, I wanted to move. I wanted a new life.

Perhaps after I moved my health would improve.

I was still seeing Y and we decided together I would move to either Oxford or Cambridge, they were both university cities, it would be easy to move now as accommodation would be easier to find. I also believed (wrongly) I was going to get well, put the past behind me, finally break away from my family. (It would be impossible to trace me once I had left London).

After a few months I would leave work it was the right time, I could not have done it before, everything in the right order, operation, move, health.

It all seemed so straightforward. Of course it was not.

Just before leaving I received a letter from my mother. Your father has just come out of his third hospital following surgery for prostate cancer. I replied that I had just come out of my thirteenth hospital after having a hysterectomy.

I expected one of her sick letters – detailing some 8-16 pages of my attitude and how I had deprived her of grandchildren etc etc etc, just a get well card. Perhaps for the second time in her life I had rendered her speechless!

Perhaps it had finally got through that I really was ill.

Either way I never had contact with or saw her again. I still had the nightmares and the memories though – they stopped the day I heard she was dead.

I went to Cambridge for the day, then Oxford. Decided I preferred Oxford so I found accommodation an area on the edge of Oxford that I was later to find was known locally as the Bermuda triangle.

For a week I was happy. I was naive, my new life was beginning.

But of course I could not leave my kidney illness behind, or my dystonia (still undiagnosed) or my medical notes with their defamatory statements. Nor people's cruelty or ignorance.

I wrote to P – she lived about twenty-five miles outside Oxford and received a welcome to your new home card, and suggested we meet soon.

How people change. I should have gone to Cambridge. Again I had made a wrong move.

Chapter 8

The Unicorn in the Garden

(One day a man was digging in his garden when he looked up and saw a unicorn chewing the grass. He went into the house and told his wife that there was a unicorn in the garden, and she told him he was mad, he should be in a looney bin, and called the police to have him sectioned. When the police arrived they asked the man, "Did you see a unicorn in the garden?"

"Of course not," said the man, "unicorns are mythical beasts and do not exist."

The police then took the wife away to the looney bin believing she was the one who was mad.)

So I moved to Oxford. I found a bedsit in a shared house. I was away from Wembley, away from people's ignorance and cruelty, out of touch with my indifferent family.

I contacted P. She seemed delighted that I had moved to Oxford and sent me a lovely welcome to your new home card, and suggested we meet soon.

Just before moving I received a letter from T. "It is disgusting the NHS have done nothing for you, until now, no wonder you kept being ill." So now she admits eight years after she left England that I WAS very ill. No apology for believing and telling everyone I was mental though.

So I was in Oxford, new life, new hope, no contact with family. I decided to leave work as soon as my face was back to normal, for a week I loved Oxford. It did not matter that I left home at six in the morning, did a full day's work in London, home at nine at night while in much pain and ill.

I had a future.

Then it started.

The imitating, the laughing the ignorance. The IC did not show, the dystonia did and in a way it was worse, (if that was possible).

I went to the John Radcliffe for tests to see if I had MS. A GP put me on antidepressants to help me cope with the ignorance, the fact that I had spent years getting off antibiotics paled into insignificance I was now back on antidepressants. Was I ever going to be free of medication?

On 18th July I wrote to P. As a homeopath, nursing sister and a good friend I hoped she would be able to help me. I spent the next few days crying, I was now ill with renal colic, cystitis, undiagnosed dystonia, wanting to sleep the pain away still going to work in London, and having to force myself to go out of the house due to others ignorance and cruelty.

Still unaware that I was well into the end stage of my disease I asked myself why my body continued to cling to life when I just wanted to die? While I waited two weeks for P to reply I kept myself going by telling myself P is your friend, she will understand, she will help. Then I phoned her. That phone call was like the shattering of a mirror. It changed my faith in human nature, my hope for the future and nearly my sanity. Whatever madness was in her mind that day I never knew and still twenty-four years later I have never discovered, and probably never will. What was it that suddenly changed love to hate and why?

"Why are you telling ME this, what do you expect ME to do about it? This cannot go on Janet, you have seen a specialist, you have had bits taken out of you, where will it end?"

"You always run away," then she said some things that made no sense.

"We know why you moved to Oxford, it was to spy on us. I have seen you looking through the windows."

Now to the rest of the world it was blindingly obvious that this woman had lost the plot, but not to me.

My friend was accusing me of the most bizarre things and obviously believed them.

It took me a few years to rationalize what was happening.

Yes I had seen a specialist – who was useless. Yes I had my womb removed – it was useless, infected, diseased and in the wrong position.

I did not 'always run away' in fact I often stayed and fought and ended up worse off. Besides if your house is on fire and the fire is out of control only a fool stays and burns, the wise man 'runs away' from it. And now of course I know the phrase 'running away' was some trendy psychobabble jargon that she had picked up.

I could not stop crying, the words 'running away' kept screaming through my brain, if I did sleep I dreamed I was running through the streets of Oxford and she was following me screaming 'running away.'

I returned to work on the Monday, well anyone else would have phoned in sick with stress, but I was not anyone else, officially there was nothing wrong with me I was not ill, I was not in pain, I was not allowed to feel. The word 'stress' then was in its infancy.

I was still in shock and started crying at work. One of the staff took me down to the nursing sister there. I was not going to tell her what was really wrong, it was private and I was still in deep shock. So I said I was afraid I had MS and I was waiting for the results of tests. She asked me what symptoms I had and then she said, "Yes you do have MS and if you do not accept my diagnosis you need psychiatric treatment."

I told her. I did not need a psychiatrist and should we not wait for the results before jumping to conclusions.

I went back to the office and had it been left there nothing more would have been said, but I was now in the hands of a hysterical woman who was convinced she was right.

In the afternoon I was called down to her again and again she told me I needed a shrink. This time I told her in no uncertain terms what I thought of the idea.

She then called down two of my work colleagues and told them I needed psychiatric treatment. One very sensibly kept quiet. But they both spent the rest of the afternoon whispering about me, looking at me and following me around. God knows what they expected me to do in the middle of an office!

Finally one told me, "You need psychiatric treatment."

I knew now what would be planned if I stayed. I was in the hands of a bunch of hysterical lunatics, if I walked out it would have been the worst thing I could have done, it would have given them an excuse to restrain me and call the emergency services, so I waited until my usual leaving time, left and never went back.

I was still in touch with Y and went straight round to her that evening.

"Maybe there is something in your friend's life that has upset her and you were the first person she spoke to."

"Maybe she is having a breakdown."

"A letter would not have had that reaction."

"She is showing signs of paranoia, these sorts of people imagine people are spying on them, or stealing."

"She is showing all the signs of Schizophrenia."

So many maybes – to other people this would have made perfect logical sense but not to me. My good friend, the only person I could trust had turned on me, made weird accusations and logic would just not penetrate.

But the next day I was laughing (briefly) when I phoned and said I would not be returning to work.

Gasps of shock from my employer when I told him where he could stick his job. I soon found out also that the nursing sister Sister M was breaking the law in diagnosing me as having MS, a nursing sister is not allowed to diagnose.

I wrote to P (on Y's advice) and said I did not understand what she was saying could we meet and discuss it? Meanwhile I made excuses for her behaviour. Hormones, menopause, or did she hate me for some reason and was trying in some strange way to end the friendship? For a week I could not eat and stayed in my room most of the time. Then when I did go out I got the shock of my life.

No one imitated me, started, laughed, or made hurtful comments. My face was back to normal. The dystonia had healed. I jumped at once to the obvious but wrong conclusion that it must be something I was eating. Food allergy. As soon as I started to eat the symptoms began again. So I began eliminating groups of foods, trying to find the culprit food. Of course it was because I had not been chewing so the mercury was not being released, but I had no idea then.

At the end of August P replied. It was one of the strangest letters I have ever received – from anyone.

"I know you are in some self created personal hell and need help to get out of it."

I need help – my God. Talk about the pot calling the kettle black! She gave me the address of a woman who was a Spiritual Counsellor and a Healer.

Why did I go? Because she knew P and I thought maybe she could make sense of what she had done and because she was a healer and I was very ill physically and would try anything that would help.

"What is behind all this?" was the first thing she said. Well I know now what was behind it. Mercury poisoning, untreated infection, kidney disease – I did try to explain I had a kidney disease – complete waste of time.

Well there was the usual useless psychobabble about 'inner child' dreams, tie cutting (a dangerous exercise as I soon found) which of course was all useless to someone with a physical disease.

This went on for three months. Three months of nightmares, not being able to eat, sleep, sometime during this period it was confirmed I did NOT have MS, or any other disease of the CNS.

Halfway through October I received a letter from my ex-firm demanding £400 in overpaid wages. By a stroke of luck I had walked out on payday (the middle of the month and paid until the end).

My reply predictably was to tell them what they could do with themselves and the beginning of many letters and a claim for constructive dismissal that ended in stalemate, and an attempt to get Sister M struck off, which ended predictably in her receiving a wrist slap and (probably) still practising.

L's sister offered me a flat in Cheltenham. Same rent I was paying for a room in Oxford. I had the chance to move away again, start again but what was the point? Everything would move with me, my IC, my dystonia. I wanted to sort things out with P first. Finally I told M (the healer/spiritual counsellor) she replied. "P would be very upset if she knew."

Well of course she bloody well knew – do you talk to a friend like that and just forget it? I had had 3 months of hell – I was upset!

2nd November 1990

We arranged to meet at the healer's house. When she arrived the first thing I heard was laughter – how could she laugh?

"Come and sit here and tell me how I have upset you."

(She did not even remember)

"I am sorry I have caused you all this hurt. Do you forgive me, I love you, I could never hate you. We will meet in the new year (1991)."

So we kept in touch and I waited for her to explain. Years of letters followed. – Too busy to meet this year, maybe next year. Or the year after, etc etc.

Today is 2/11/14 – I have never seen her since, she never explained.

It took me two years to get over what she did, I had to move back to London to do it.

I even forgave her but I have never forgotten, nor can I ever completely trust anyone. P taught me an important lesson. The only person you can ever trust fully is yourself.

Chapter 9

The Snake Pit

December 1990-Sept 1992

So I moved to Cheltenham. New beginning, new home, my own front door. Here I could forget Oxford. Moving there had been a mistake. Not moving back to London was to be an even bigger one.

I had the flat I always wanted. I was away from my family, they would would never find me here. I was away from my old firm and I had a horrible incurable disease which I did not know I was in the end stage of, or what it was called, or the fact I had been lied to.

Again in my naive way I thought things were going to improve. How? Who was going to employ someone with a severe kidney disease and a twisted face. The only work I could face was something where I did not meet the public, so I was employed as a cleaner, as a temporary measure until I was well. I would never have contemplated this work until now, for me the only way now was up – things could not get any worse.

It was not too bad, students and lecturers were friendly as were the other women, S was kind, and for a few months I thought that things may improve.

Wrong again, my then undiagnosed dystonia was getting worse. The pain was getting worse. (I should now have been living on morphine to control it).

So back to a doctor for antidepressants. He gave me amitriptyline. Now these at least began to knock the edge off the pain of the IC (a side effect of these drugs.) But now I had swapped antibiotics for antidepressants, was I going to spend my life on pills? While all the time I could hear P's voice 'running away again.'

I was of course still in touch with P, still believing we would meet, still believing she would explain and we could be friends again.

When I wrote to her I lied, because that is what she wanted to hear. She was kind if she thought I was doing what she said, believing what she wanted me to believe.

On my birthday I received a lovely card, a promise we would meet, she wanted to come to see me, to see my flat, and a present, a book. She had been ill, and the book had helped her. Now this book became a best seller and I did try to read it and things began to make sense. I have in my life read books that are rubbish. This one was not only rubbish, it was dangerous rubbish. According to LH all disease comes from the mind and you can think yourself well – what it said about cancer I will not repeat but if P, a supposedly intelligent woman, actually believed this crap then no wonder she accused people of spying on her! I used the book first to prop up the wonky leg of my kitchen table, then later tore it to shreds which was definitely therapeutic!

I was now down to seven stone in weight, in intolerable pain, living on antidepressants to stop me killing myself, and to try to take the edge off the pain, only going out to work partly due to people's negative reactions to my dystonia and partly because walking hurt so much, due to the uncontrolled pelvic pain.

So towards the end of May I contacted a homeopathic

doctor, a female I explained about the IC/cystitis (undiagnosed) about the oromandibular dystonia (undiagnosed).

"It's all emotional, you will need long-term therapy," she said.

I walked out into the sunshine and left her in her weird little world.

It is not only the orthodox medical profession who breed quacks, the Alternative/Complementary world has its share.

The flat I was living in had been on the market for two years, now it was being sold so I found another flat in Cheltenham. My next practitioner was a Kinesiologist – I consulted her about the dystonia, "It's a problem with your liver, it's not functioning properly," she said.

Yes, the liver can affect the jaw and could have been the cause of my dystonia – it was not.

Back home in my flat I spent a week crying, going to work, coming home swallowing pills and not eating and I began to feel I was in a snake pit. Deep at the base of the pit and the snakes were outside, they had faces of people I knew.

'We are waiting for you', they were saying, 'there is no point in climbing out, we will get you.' I could not sleep, I wanted to die but again something made me go on. I knew that if I gave in someone would have me sectioned – because of course my disease was officially non-existent. I was a head case.

So I hid it all, my physical pain, my emotional pain, everything because as I have always found – it's safer.

It had been a year now since that phone call that had turned my life upside down.

P still kept in touch, now she had found a new hobby

'opening up to the universe', no wonder she had gone off the rails – consciously it all made sense, subconsciously I still heard 'running away' in my head. Then the letters began.

'Sorry we did not have time to see you this year, maybe next year.'

The first of many letters, excuse after excuse, year after year. Too busy, push Janet to the back, relatives first, friends first, too busy. One day at work I passed out with the pain. Not the first time it had happened but this time I had a witness and no one could say I imagined it. My boss was concerned so I told her I had seen a doctor about it and her reply was, "Oh good, it is nothing serious is it, that will put your mind at rest."

No, nothing serious, just so much pain I pass out, should be on morphine, suffering from an end stage disease but officially nothing was wrong so nothing serious.

Still believing my IC and dystonia could be diet related I tried cutting out foods that I believed were causing it. It did not work of course, I was in the end stage, it would not have worked but believing I was doing everything I could kept me going, kept me sane, gave me hope.

In December 1991 while cleaning an office I got talking to a lady who was interested in Alternative/ Complementary medicine. "That is what I would love to do, but I have no qualifications," I said. (Then at least an A level in Biology and Chemistry were needed for most colleges.) Also I was too ill to travel to college and study.

B was studying to be a homeopath and explained there were some courses where you do not need qualifications. B gave me a prospectus and luckily the nutrition course did not need A levels. I chose to work by correspondence course as travelling from Cheltenham to London was impossible due to my illness.

I had something to live for, something good would come out of all the suffering and illness. Little did I know then that it would take so long and I was to achieve a goal that some days seemed worthless. I did not go out unless I had to. Pain, illness, my dystonia – I stayed in that flat, and studied. I dreamed of the day when I was qualified. Even if I was too ill to go out to work, I could work from home. I could help people with cystitis/IC, my life would one day have a meaning. Some good would come from all of this suffering.

Yet still, bouts when I was on amitryptiline, afraid to go out because of peoples ignorance.

I now knew I was suffering from dystonia. A female doctor in Cheltenham had confirmed my disease was physical, told me it was called dystonia and pronounced me incurable in one sentence. I was not offered any treatment. Botox was never mentioned, she refused to give me muscle relaxants, refused to give me anything. So now I had TWO horrible incurable diseases.

Having proof that my disease was physical and had a name is no help when people are so ignorant. Sick of the imitating, name-calling, being shouted after etc I knew that my sanity was being threatened. I knew I would never get over what P had done unless I moved back to London, and put the last two years behind me. I had learned a valuable lesson. Sort your health and any other problems out first, if not they just move with you.

So back to London. I rented a room the size of a cupboard in Mornington Crescent north London. L thought I was mad. "Why did you leave when you had a lovely flat and now you are in a room the size of a box?" Of course I never told her why. Never told her I was on the verge of a breakdown because of my ill health because I could not forget P.

I knew what the reaction would be. Headcase/ psychiatrist etc because of course there was nothing officially physically wrong.

(I found in May 2002 that 19 months of my medical notes – Dec 1990 – July 1992 have mysteriously disappeared. This included my diagnosis of dystonia.)

Chapter 10

Bleeding Moon

I met S on 2nd Sept 1992 and we have been friends ever since.

S was a hypnotherapist. Not that for a minute I believed that any part of my disease was psychological or psycho anything. I had gone to S in the hope that she would help me with the food allergies, and to stick to the diets as I still believed allergy was playing quite a big part in my symptoms. Actually it was only playing a small part then, but I did not know that.

I was expecting my therapist to be a man so it was surprising to meet a woman, and one who had some sense and understood straight away that the problem was physical. We did not discuss my IC, just allergies.

During those first months at her Harley Street clinic we soon worked out that the cause was not allergy/ stress/ etc the cause was a mystery, for three years but I carried on with the hypnosis, and from this followed a friendship, a career, and happiness. I stayed in Camden for five years.

Under hypnosis up came the memories of the physical and mental abuse, and I went back to the night of the attempted murder and found my father was there but not involved, and the experience of going back (quite unplanned) into my past life.

The mental pain began to heal, I was not used to kindness, someone saying 'let me give you a hug' and during those months I began to get over what P had done but physically nothing changed.

In March 1993 I consulted an Iridologist in London, "You could have Myasthenia Gravis," she told me.

Now I had consulted her mainly about my oromandibular dystonia, not my undiagnosed IC. But she missed the blindingly obvious.

Also part of the Nutrition course I was studying included Iridology my first class was a weekend in May 1993 I was living on amitriptyline for the pain,

I now had two incurable diseases to contend with – but neither was cancer so it did not matter did it?

S treated me like a normal sane human being – which was a change from the way most people treated me! She sent me to a doctor she knew in London who sent me to a specialist at the Hospital for Nervous diseases in London – who promptly told me there was nothing wrong with me.

It is said that the darkest hour is just before dawn. This has been proved twice in my life once here in July 1993 when two things happened.

My mind split in two and I found the cause of my disease.

For two weeks I was in another world. Luckily I was unemployed at the time and did not have to go to work and pretend. I was looking down on a body that was swallowing paracetamol after paracetamol and not caring what happened, willing my sick diseased body to die, my body down there knew exactly what I was doing even if I didn't, it would not die. I drank, took pills, but it refused even to react.

Now I knew that amitriptyline and alcohol together would kill me, but if it did not work then I would end up with appalling brain damage so I was not that far gone. I kept off the amis.

My body refused to die, it had been so drugged up with antibiotics, painkillers, anything I could get my hands on and it would NOT die.

I came through that 2 weeks on my own in silence cursing the fact that I was still alive, and thankful that I had been on my own so that no one could call in the shrinks and label me mental for daring to believe I would be better off dead.

I went ahead with the second half of the Iridology course, for one reason only. I had paid for it and anyone who knows me knows that I get my money's worth. Even if I would rather be dead!

My mind was still on automatic pilot, I was still drifting through each day, then on 23rd August 1993 I found the cause of my disease which had been missed by doctors, specialists, consultants and even an Iridologist.

In my right iris was a bright orange mark in the area that corresponds to the jaw. One of the causes of these marks is heavy metal deposits. In my jaw on the side the muscles of my mouth moved towards was a large mercury filling. I was not nuts, my disease was not psychosomatic, or psycho anything. My dystonia was caused by mercury poisoning, and how does the body get rid of this highly toxic poison? Through the kidneys!

All I had to do was have the filling removed, my dystonia would clear up and my kidney disease would heal.

How simple, how naive – I sat in St James's Park – dreaming of a future, dreaming of being free of pain, of passing my exams, of practicing as an Alternative Practitioner. All I had to do now was find a dentist to take out the filling. But of course it is not that easy. Life never is! It took me nearly a year to find a dentist who would take me seriously and luckily I found a good one in Harley Street. Anthony Newbury (now deceased) was a famous mercury free dentist. I was tested first for mercury poisoning the levels from 1 – safe to 9 – dead. My result was level 8!

I was treated by Alan Hibberd a famous clinical ecologist for removal of the mercury. Dr Hibberd explained that all my dystonia symptoms were due to mercury poisoning and 50% of my kidney symptoms and IC were due to it, also the other 50% of my IC was due to untreated infection.

When I look back now of course it all made sense. The extensive dental treatment when I was twelve. The first signs of kidney disease at 13, it should have been obvious to a ten year old child. Pity the NHS does not employ ten year old children.

Also I remember a conversation with a consultant MANY years ago at a London hospital it would have been in the early 1970s when he asked me.

"Do you have any mercury fillings in your teeth?"

"Yes I have one."

Then nothing else was said – or checked – or questioned and I dismissed it as an odd question. Did he suspect? Why did he ask? Why was nothing done? Of course I believed wrongly that now it would be all plain sailing. Remove filling, have chelation treatment to remove mercury, body well.

First due to the fact that my kidneys were inflamed and badly damaged the treatment had to be slowed down considerably, otherwise it would have killed me. Secondly I had no idea I had IC, much less that I was in the end stage.

As the treatment started it made my IC symptoms worse (if that was possible) as the mercury irritated the kidneys and bladder as it passed through.

On 28th April 1995 I saw my first IC client in Mornington

Crescent via a letter I had written to the COB Foundation. By some bizarre twist of fate is was five years later to the day that I was finally diagnosed. I did not know then how ill I was, only that I wanted to help others with this devastating disease. I was qualified with a diploma in Nutrition by now and full of dreams for the future, despite my illness and pain, I was going to practice from home if I had to but I was going to practice I was going to help others through this.

Pauline had been ill for forty years, she was in her sixties and wanted to die. (I didn't blame her). Before she left she said to me, "You are the only person in forty years who has understood or given me any hope thank you."

I was at the time starting, just starting to feel a little better. I kept telling myself your body will heal now. Riding the pain, riding the bad days when I felt too ill to go out of the house.

This is what all the studying was for, this is what all the essays, waiting for the marks, the results was all about. I was going to heal.

The chelation treatment continued until February 1996. I know the exact date it finished as it is on my medical notes, the only reference on my notes to the fact that I was poisoned by mercury.

FIVE YEARS of my notes have disappeared. (Another coincidence!)

My friendship with S continued. S was kind, she understood pain she understood illness, (having been through a lot herself) we went to what I believed was a healing circle. Which I found out when I arrived was a clairvoyant circle.

One of the group K, went into a trance and described what he saw, "Does it mean anything to you?" he asked.

"No," I said. It did. He had described very clearly a

bladder in the very end stages of IC! Obviously he did not have a clue what it was – clairvoyants only pass on what they see. There is no way he could have guessed, made it up. It had to be true. But of course I denied it. It was something else. It had to be. It was too weird. Even though I knew I would not admit. But of course I could not keep that information to myself for too long. Back on amis for the pain and to stop me killing myself. I told S.

"Don't worry it's a healing crisis," she said, "we all got the same."

I admitted I was in intolerable pain and she taught me how to control it a little using hypnosis. "Don't top yourself now, we are going out next week." She understood, understood how bad pain and illness can be understood how low it can make you feel.

In June 1997 I went to the Spiritual Association of Great Britain to consult a healer, V, for the first time.

And in July I met XX.

Two hours of strange conversation later including her telling me that she was the expert, (no one had suffered like she had) I had no right to be treating people with Cystitis as she knew it all, had no right to work with patients with mercury poisoning SHE was the expert, etc etc, there is no such thing as IC all cystitis is caused by germs from the bowel, outside in etc etc talk about bedside manner absent!

BUT she did put me in touch with the London Clinic and Doctor L and finally after TWENTY YEARS of wrong tests, wrong antibiotics, the germ that was causing my 'imaginary' disease was identified. STREP F – a bug that lives in the intestines and is lethal in causing UTI. Why had it not been discovered? Because no-one had had the common sense to test for it.

To add insult to injury, it responded to penicillin, the one antibiotic I had always said was the one that did any good and the only one the NHS would not prescribe because they believed it was wrong. You couldn't make it up!

On top of that the tests nearly didn't happen. XX attitude to clinic staff was abysmal, "Don't you know who I am I am XX?" I left the clinic while they were still going at it hammer and tongs. Luckily Dr L still saw me.

S meanwhile had gone away for a week and was staying at her home looking after her dog. The penicillin had started to work I was feeling a lot better then the course finished. Then the infection came back – it was a Saturday afternoon and I was walking round the countryside looking for a doctor – any doctor I could get an emergency prescription from and very angry that the NHS had not had the common sense to do a simple urine test twenty years ago.

On the Monday I crawled back to my GP only to find he was on holiday. Well it did not matter, a doctor is a doctor and this one was a woman. "There is nothing wrong with you, you have urethral syndrome," she announced.

I had heard enough. "Don't be so bloody silly, you have never met me you know NOTHING about my medical history, and you have only seen me for two minutes."

"I will have to wait until the notes arrive then see what tests you have had."

"Every bloody test in the book, except the one that would have detected the right bug, now can I have the antibitoics."

"No."

"Why not?"

"Because it is dangerous to keep taking antibiotics."

"I know that, I could write a bloody book on the dangers I was given the wrong ones for twenty years."

I then told her about the mercury poisoning and the

fact that it had not been detected for twenty years.

"It's not their fault."

"Are you defending the mistakes of thirteen NHS consultants?"

"Yes, it is not their fault as mercury poisoning is not routine."

I left then as I had a very strong desire to smash my fist into her face, and spent five weeks off work with a severe kidney infection. When my GP returned he actually admitted she was wrong. I asked to see my medical notes and he was quite co-operative and it was then he discovered that seven years of the notes had mysteriously disappeared. AGAIN!

"I'd like them FOUND!" I replied, "it's strange that at a time it is discovered that the cause of my disease has been found the notes disappear isn't it?" He agreed.

Well to cut a long story short letters went back and fourth, nothing was done, notes were lost then I threatened to take legal action. I received a letter by return of post notes found.

Suggestion – if you want action with the NHS just say solicitor – it works!

Meanwhile S was organising a project in London and I was to help she suggested I saw a homeopath she knew.

At first the woman was sympathetic, then things changed.

"It's all down to anger," she said, "it is due to the abuse you received as a child," she started quoting form the book (now famous) by LH and suggested I go on an anger management course, a course on how to manage anger! A course on how to avoid quacks would have been more useful.

I was now working at the Spiritualist Association of Great Britain Clinic.

I was only working mornings at the moment so I was able to work at the SAGB in London on Wednesday afternoons as a voluntary worker at the healing clinic. I was a receptionist, I loved the work, I was having healing every Wednesday and V was good to me.

Another person understood what it was like to be so ill and in so much pain, and was helping me.

I was still studying for my Diploma in Dietary Therapeutics (the last one to qualify as a nutritionist). Then the letter arrived.

'Earlier this year we attended the winding up of your late mother's estate. Following which your father-------.'

I had to read it several times. Not the bit that my father was dead and that he had left me a large legacy but the former part. My mother was dead. No more would she spread lies saying I was mental. No more would she tell people I imagined illness and pain. The woman who had hated me, tried to kill me, lied about me was dead. The nightmares that I had continually for over twenty years stopped. She could never hurt me again.

Now IF my disease had been caused by abuse and the attempted murder technically my body should now have started to heal – it didn't.

Still being very ill and unable to travel far the solicitor agreed to meet me in Exeter, (as far as it was possible for me to travel by train). I learned that I would be very well off. I could buy a flat, I could buy anything I liked, I thought financially I would be set up for life. It meant little to me. All I wanted was my HEALTH. I would have given it away the next day if I could swap it for my health.

Chapter 11

Don't Mention Healing

I had found an IC group in London – the only one apparently. Why did I go? Well I thought I may be able to help, someone might be interested. When I had written a letter in 1997 in the Cob Foundation magazine 25 ladies had contacted me asking me about the mercury connection and I had replied to all 25 giving them details of testing, chelation treatment etc.

A year later I wrote again to all 25 – five replied. Two admitted they had not done anything about it. One had found her IC was due to Candida allergy and two had gone ahead, had their fillings removed and their IC was at that point dramatically improved.

So I went along hopeful I could help, even if I could not help myself. That evening I was feeling particularly bad and on arrival when asked how I was I admitted I was not feeling very well.

"I hope you are not bringing bad luck with you." What a way to greet someone! Well I tried.

One of the ladies there who I could have helped if she had bothered to listen was rude. She demanded a diet specific to IC (there isn't one) as I tried to explain diets are individual. When I left a lady who left with me said the same as me. "Well I won't be going back there again!" Her first and last time. I vowed then I would one day have a group of my own – and I would never speak to anyone in the way I had been spoken to!

Meanwhile V who had kept me going every Wednesday, giving me hope and healing, arranged an appointment with a Harley Street doctor she knew.

He was the usual unhelpful moron. The X-ray showed I had medullary sponge kidney – but it is all right, you are not going to die, and it is not affecting your life is it?

No I am quite happy having IC, being in constant pain, feeling permanently ill, having no life but I am not going to bloody die so that is OK.

"What causes it?"

"Untreated UTI."

(I assume in my case the one that does not exist!)

V was disgusted and took me to a healer she knew in London, again a Harley Street Doctor.

"It's fantastic that you are a healer as well as a doctor," I told him, "you will be able to help so many patients."

"It isn't," he replied. "If it was known I was also working as a healer I would be struck off."

(This is not the only time I have met this strange attitude in the orthodox medical profession. I had the same conversation with a doctor at the Royal Alexandra Children's Hospital in 2001. Obviously the point of doctors is not to heal!

I loved the receptionist job I talked to the patients, really believed my career in Alternative medicine had begun, I was doing the work I wanted to do, working through the pain and illness, the work gave me something to live for.

May 1998

I was due to go with S to a lecture in a hotel somewhere

118

in the country. I was ill, in much pain, and trying to hide it as usual.

Eventually I gave in said I had to go home I was too ill and in too much pain.

"Maybe there is somewhere you can lie down," said S.

Lie down, give in admit I was ill and in pain! Now looking back it sounds unbelievable – then that is the way it was.

I had been programmed to ignore pain, pretend it did not exist, put up with it because it was not there I 'imagined' it. Or I was not going to die so that was OK.

For a while I joined the real world. Real people do not pretend pain does not exist. Soon after this I became ill with kidney infection, running a temperature, something was obviously wrong. In desperation I phoned doctor L at the London clinic where I had attended last year.

"Come round straight away." Straight away – how different is private medicine to the NHS! I jumped into a passing taxi arrived in a few minutes and commented to his secretary how easy it had been to get an appointment.

"Things move in the private sector," she laughed.

Dr L was a normal human doctor (there are a few in this country)

He complained to ME about the failing of the NHS, explained NHS tests often show false negative results and doctors KNEW this.

Told me St Peter's was one of the worst hospitals in England for incompetent doctors NOW I find out.

He sent me for tests – the germ could not be isolated but at least he tried, he believed me, he admitted my disease existed.

I was due to see Dr L again and needed a letter from my GP. I had given her a week's notice and returned that morning to collect the letter, on the way to see him.

"I haven't got the notes," said bitch, "just a letter from A Hibberd. I can't give you that."

I explained through gritted teeth that the notes were needed by Dr L and the letter from A Hibberd, I was on my way to see Dr L she had had a week.

"Well you can go and get a photocopy of this letter, there is a machine in the shop down the road."

I told her it was NOT my job to do HER work, the appointment with Dr L was in an hour and if I stopped to do HER work I would be late.

"I haven't got the notes."

"Your receptionist outside has them, I will get them and bring them in."

While I was getting the notes she called the next patient in.

I marched back into the room, slammed the notes on her desk, told her what she could do with the letter, and what I thought of the NHS in general which was heard in the waiting room, to the delight of the waiting patients and the receptionist who told me she is always doing this.

I arrived at Dr L's with just the X-rays and no letter.

Dr L was furious and wanted to write a letter of complaint about her.

He looked at the X-rays, told me I had a refluxing ureter which is KNOWN to cause infection.

"Can you operate?" I asked.

"No need, all you have to do to stop it is sleep with your upper body raised." He explained that when you sleep the bladder is at a higher level than the kidneys and if you have this condition, sleeping at this angle prevents the urine backing up to the kidneys.

"Why was I not told this all those years ago years ago, it is so simple."

"It's because it is simple no one told you."

So twelve years ago I could so easily have corrected this 12 years of unnecessary infection because no one pointed it out!

In July 1998 I received the cheque for the money my father had left.

Now anyone who has money of that amount left to them would be as happy as if they had won the lottery. It meant nothing to me. I wanted to be free of pain, to be well, to have a life and a future. Money is no good when you are so ill you are hoping to die.

A short period of happiness followed (not due to the money) I was working at SAGB people cared about me people wanted to help, I would soon pass my exams I dreamed of being a Nutritionist, and I dreamed of something positive coming out of all the illness and suffering.

Chapter 12

The Evil in the garden?

V. SAGB "Whatever you try to do a door is slammed in your face."

Yes V saw my life the way it was. Door after door, time after time.

For a few months I went into remission. I did not know then that this was quite normal with IC, I did not know I even had IC.

I only know that the pain eased, I felt much better and I believed that the healing was working.

I had moved to Archway. Working at a college in Holloway.

For over 5 months I had been feeling so much better, this was it my body after 25 years of pain and illness was beginning to heal.

Then in July 1999 my final diploma arrived. I had reached my goal I was now a qualified to practice Dietary Therapeutics. I had enough money to set me up for life (or so I thought). This was it – at last. I was going to get well! But that tiny voice, 'I am always here. I am your disease. I will never leave you.'

Then in August 1999 the pain returned. The holiday was over. At first I thought nothing of it, a healing crisis, in fact it was a disease crisis, the disease was in the ascent. With the pain and illness came the despair again.

Just a weekend off, just a small holiday – back to work, back to normal! Hide the pain, don't show how you feel. Just get on with it. So I did, the pain got worse I felt more ill. More depressed. No hope. I could not keep phoning S or V. It was MY pain my illness. I did not need to work as a cleaner, I had enough money and more to live on. I could just give up work crawl home, wait to die. I was getting up for work at 4.30, 40 minute walk to work to clean when I did not need to.

I told my boss (male) I did not want to work at college anymore.

Being male he completely misunderstood. "Talk to E," he suggested.

E was my supervisor, female and not I thought the type of person to talk to.

"What is the problem, talk to E." Yes I wanted to talk to someone who would understand, someone who would say yes you need to be in hospital, you need an operation, this can't go on. They have to do something about the pain. Simple, logical but my life was not simple and logical, my disease was not simple and logical (it did not officially exist). If I had cancer it would have been easier, people understand that.

"I can't take anymore," I said, sounding like the village idiot.

"What can't you take, life? Work?"

"Work. I want to give up cleaning." Which was not of course what I meant to say.

"OK."

The next day I really was too ill to work so I phoned her.

"I cannot work today I am too ill and in too much pain."

"OK, no problem."

No problem, I was allowed to say I was in pain, allowed to be ill, allowed to stay off work and this was no problem!

All my life I had been told, 'is that all that is wrong with you? You must go to work or you will lose your job' etc and now I was learning it was OK to be ill. I went to work the next day still in intolerable pain. I was crying with the pain and E said to me, "You are ill, you are not yourself, why don't you see a doctor?"

Then it hit me. E thought I had a mental problem, she thought I was suffering from depression! Well I was not having that. I explained that my disease was purely PHYSICAL.

"Go home, you will be paid until the end of the week, I will give you my mobile number, phone me if you have a problem."

I was not used to this, E was understanding, being sympathetic, caring. Was this real?

18th September 1999

Tonight I had a dream. I was walking in the centre of a garden, there was a man with a large stick in his hand. He threw the stick into the air, and as it came towards me it turned into a long straight snake. As it landed at my feet I woke up.

I felt stabbing, swords knives – I was being shown cutting and central London. I was awake this time. Sitting at the desk in SAGB. I was in the garden again, and in the centre was a clear pool. A man was holding my body above the pool and blood was dripping from it into the pool, the man was saying. "You are all right, you are not dead, just injured."

The pain became worse, my illness became worse and I was back on amis for the pain, I tracked down a doctor I had seen privately in London a few years ago, now working at Roehampton Hospital and asked if it was possible to operate.

"No one in this country will remove a kidney while it is still working," he told me. "Why?"

"Because they are taught not to at medical college," he replied.

So I had a kidney disease, right kidney, refluxing ureter right kidney, continual infection, right kidney and they would not perform an obvious needed operation. In this country.

Solution – go abroad.

Why not – now it is much easier to get surgery abroad, then this process was in its infancy. I was not computer literate, had no idea where to start. For obvious reasons had no one to advise me. But I kept this at the forefront of my mind – and it kept me sane.

I was feeling suicidal again. I phoned S. See Dr C, my doctor in London. So I did, he gave me SSRI. "He's given me antidepressants," I said to S. "Why, when he knows now my disease is physical?"

S did not understand this either and phoned him.

"He did not know what else to do."

A letter arrived from Dr R Roehampton with the name of a specialist.

The specialist just wanted to repeat the tests I had had many times before.

In December V gave me the address of a doctor she knew in London. A brilliant man, sympathetic, listened, explained that my kidneys were not filtering the blood properly and also confirmed I had refluxing ureter, which is why I kept getting kidney infections.

Finally he made the most sensible remark I had heard in over twenty years.

You need a FEMALE urologist.

The millennium. Most people can remember what they

were doing on 1st January 2000 (if they were not too drunk!) So can I. I was lying down in intolerable pain feeling very ill, wanting to die. The day passed in a haze of drugged sleep to blot out the pain. I was again too ill to work. On my return on the way to work I met E "How are you? Are you alright darling?" Those few kind words prevented me from taking the massive overdose I had planned to take that weekend.

I had entered the year that was going to bring unimaginable hell at first then the end of my disease. Had I not met E I would now be dead.

23rd January 2000

The painkillers did not even touch the pain. It is a freezing cold night, all I have to do is go out lay down in the local park and freeze to death, something stopped me. Not so much hope, but the fact that I was allowed to be ill, to feel, admit I was ill, to admit I was in pain, to admit I felt down and because at last there were people in my life who gave a damn.

So I stayed inside and the next day wrote off for addresses of female consultants. It turned out there were only 8 female urologists in England and 4 of those were retired. I wrote to the four. Three had moved on – I had an appointment with the fourth.

JM was one of the kindest most positive people I have ever met.

"Why haven't you had kidney scans, you should have had them 20 years ago?"

"Yes there is a chance that the kidney can be removed, it depends on the results of the scans."

20th March 2000

Scans showed one kidney smaller than the other but nothing else – then came the bad news. "It could be IC."

It was not possible, my symptoms were not those of IC. I had treated IC patients, I had done case histories on ladies with IC, I believed she was wrong and I knew there was no known cure for IC. Besides, I had had 4 cystoscopies they were hardly likely to miss IC! I told her no tests, no treatment I did not want to know.

"Think it over," she told me.

I spent 3 days, crying, shaking in shock – she was wrong.

I called S, "If you do not have the tests you will never know," she told me. And S was right I could not just leave it hanging in the air. I phoned E and told her I was going into hospital, "OK mate."

25th April 2000

I cannot believe now looking back that when I went into hospital that day to hear the worst news of my life, I actually went to work that morning.

But that is typical JB. The world goes on turning, the sun goes on shining the rest of the world carries on regardless.

"Let me know how you get on, hope everything is OK."

I was almost happy. E cared, V cared, S cared.

28th April 2000

Today my life was going to change. Today was the beginning of my healing. Tomorrow my life would start. Tomorrow would see the beginning of the end of my suffering. The needle was put into my hand. I fell asleep.

Chapter 13

Hell

7:30pm 28th April 2000

AND WOKE UP IN HELL

You do have IC it is in the end stage – but don't worry, it is not cancer, it won't kill you.

So that is all right then, isn't it? I have a horrible disabling, painful disease. I will eventually end up housebound, probably bedridden, under morphine. But it is not cancer, and won't kill me so that is all right. ARENT I LUCKY! My reply that I would be better off with end stage cancer, at least they would operate or I would die but I would not be left in limbo I am sure shocked her. GOOD it was meant to. "Will you operate and give me a cystectomy?" I asked.

"No."

"Why not?"

"Because you do not have cancer."

Well I refuse to just exist, I want my life back and I will not accept that due to the incompetence of the NHS this is how it is going to be left.

Her words at the following consultation should have shocked me. The results from the laboratory had shocked her. I had been in end stage IC (the worse case she had ever seen) for OVER TWENTY YEARS.

"HOW did they miss it?"

"WHY did they miss it?"

No one had MISSED anything. It was obvious to me that there had been an almighty cock up and an even bigger cover up.

Two things had to be done now…

1. operate
2. find out the truth.

The third option was to end my life because I had no intention of spending it just existing in intolerable pain and illness courtesy of the NHS.

30ᵗʰ April 2000

Drugged sleep, sedation (my own every time I surfaced I took anything I could lay my hands on).

I phoned V. "You will get well," she told me.

And she was right. Thank God someone had not given up.

I wrote to JM and told her she MUST operate or do something I would rather be dead than suffer like this. And I meant it. Also I had taken a big risk. Even hint at suicide to the NHS and they all run around like headless chickens screaming psychiatrist/counselling/etc. Well JM had compassion and also a rare commodity in the orthodox medical profession – common sense. She knew this was not a threat, but a promise.

5ᵗʰ May 2000

I phoned E and said I wished to give 2 weeks' notice at work.

Whatever was going to happen I was not going to waste what was left of my life in a dead end cleaning job when I did not need to.

E, "What is wrong?"

"I have been told I am incurably ill."

"I will see you Wednesday, we will have a little chat I do not want to lose you."

Wednesday came. There was no little chat, I wanted to thank her for being one of the few people in my life who had cared – I didn't, she would probably think I was nuts.

I saw JM again on 15th May 2000. She refused to operate it – was too risky. I could die (as if it mattered). She gave me a prescription for Elmiron then the supposed new wonder drug for IC which was highly toxic, only was supposed to work in the early stages and was the most expensive drug in the world at £1,000 per prescription.

She never knew I did not take it and I make no apologies for lying and telling her I did.

Elmiron was soon found to be not much use, made your hair fall out and made patients sick, (even if the price of it did come down considerably.)

S phoned, "I don't believe you will not get well. A (her partner) is looking it up on the internet."

22nd May 2000

I am 48 today, incurably ill and I want to die, happy birthday!

Somehow I lived through the hell, God knows how. Probably by staying in shock. Trendy psychobabblists would call it "denial". I called it hope! And I planned to

130

move to Brighton. I had enough money (or so I thought) to be financially independent for the rest of my life. I could buy anything I wanted, my own flat, do anything I wanted, my abuser was dead, and I was incurably ill and wanted to die. It was funny. Sick but funny.

I kept going down to Brighton to buy a flat that I now had no interest in, and would never live in, as I was going to die. Why? Because it was what I had always wanted. It got me through the day alive, and took my mind off what was happening and kept me sane. It was a weird game I was playing to get me through each day – and it worked.

9th June 2000

I was very ill with another kidney infection and bacterial cystitis and IC yet I was discussing my 'future' with a mortgage advisor. We decided that I would have to put down a very large deposit, as they did not usually give mortgages to part time cleaners who have a serious illness, no matter how much they have financially.

Even if I was qualified as an alternative complementary medicine therapist I was always seen officially as a cleaner.

10th June 2000

I wrote to JM asking for date of operation or forget it, I was sick of playing games.

22nd June 2000

So ill all the time now. The flat is going ahead and I could not care less.

For so long I dreamed of living in Sussex, now I feel nothing.

26th June 2000

"Yes I will operate."

I found out it was not me who swayed her, but when she had been on a conference abroad she had met a lady who had said, "Operate, you will change her life."

I never found out who this lady was but I would like to thank her. I owe my life and health to her also. I left the hospital on air. At last the operation I had waited twenty years for was to happen. I also was more ill than ever.

It was as if the disease was having a last fling. I am still here – you haven't got rid of me yet. I phoned V and told her the good news.

Her reply surprised me.

She was shocked I would consider such a drastic operation, and the cost of it. V had been giving me healing for 3 years she knew how ill I was and she was shocked?

8th July 2000

A booklet arrived giving details of the operation. Details I would like to have done without. I would rather have just gone in blind, got on with it and worked through the rest later.

Panic/revulsion and fear of the epidural, that something would go wrong and I would end up paralysed from the waist down. Knowing my luck.

8th August 2000

I went to the hospital for pre-op tests. Everyone was very kind, but very shocked that I wanted such a drastic operation, when I did not have cancer.

Chapter 14

Well

11th August 2000

Admission day.

On the way to the tube E drove by and stopped.
   "What are you doing here?"
   "Going to hospital for major surgery."
   "Fingers crossed."
   "When you are better come and see me."
   I travelled to that hospital in a fog. I did not need drugs to get me in this time. The fear had gone, I knew it was going to be all right. Someone cared – just those few words changed everything.

12th August 2000 8.30 am

Needle in the hand. My bladder was removed. A miracle. No more pain. No more illness, no more suffering. It could never come back. Twenty years to the day I was told I was incurable at the London Homeopathic, I WAS WELL.

14th August 2000

L and Z visited me. S kept joking – I did not need cheering

up. I was ecstatic. I dreamed about my future my career, Brighton, my flat, Sussex.

Everyone was kind and caring. The consultant came to see me every day

After leaving hospital I stayed with L for a few weeks then back home to London.

Obviously like every new urostomate I experienced a few minor problems. "Don't worry." said my stoma nurse, "all new patients have a few problems you are adjusting very well." And the bag was a small price to pay for having a life and health.

I saw E again briefly in Dec 2000 just after I moved to Sussex in November. I still remember that time and how a woman who was almost a stranger gave me the will and hope to go on living. With just a few kind words.

Part Two

Chapter 15

The Truth Will Out

The euphoria continued for five months. I was in Sussex, where I always longed to be. My career could start, I could help others with the same disease. Most of all I was WELL.

I could sleep all night – something I had not been able to do for thirty years.

I had my first Christmas free of pain and illness. I looked forward to a holiday – something I had given up at least twenty years ago. Most of all was the knowledge that my disease could NEVER return it was not in remission it had GONE. I woke up each day, glad to be alive. Well into January 2001.

Then I started to ask questions, I began to ask WHY. WHY had they missed it? How did they miss it? DID they miss it? Anger began to replace euphoria. My next project was to get to the TRUTH.

Meanwhile I tried to get work in a clinic, or work from home, advertised in Sussex. Tried to get my career I had worked on for so long off the ground.

I had assumed that Sussex was not like London, there were a few clinics, a few practices, finding work would be easy.

I soon found that no clinic wanted an Iridologist, and no one wanted a newly qualified nutritionist either. All wanted someone with at least two years working experience.

So I began work as a cleaner at the Royal Alexandra Children's Hospital. This did not bother me, it was a children's hospital. Maybe someone there would be interested in Alternative/Complementary therapy. Not a chance.

In the two years I worked there I met a doctor who was a healer and must not admit it. The same reply as in London. "You must be joking if I say I am a healer or try to heal here I would be struck off! That sort of thing is not wanted here!"

Eventually I did find out there was a small group interested in Complementary therapy but it was kept very quiet.

The head of a children's clinic used to come to the meetings so I asked him if there was any chance of my working there. Same answer, they would not consider anyone with less than two years working experience.

Also there was so much, we have to ask permission for this, get this cleared go through this procedure etc I don't know if any clinic ever got off the ground, but if it had I knew it would have taken ten years and I hadn't got ten years.

Meanwhile I was searching for the truth about my medical notes. I was advised by someone at the Royal Alexandra, "Don't go to your GP they will remove what they do not want you to see, go straight to a solicitor." Good advice and very true.

So in September 2001 I consulted one locally who dealt with medical negligence claims.

M could not have been more helpful, she was also sympathetic, as suspected some of the notes had 'disappeared', also luckily she got everything moving just before the case became statute barred.

Dr JM also wrote that although she would not get involved with litigation she did put in writing that the disease had wrecked my life.

My medical notes made interesting, if offensive reading.

I knew things that had been written were not exactly complimentary but on reading some of the lies it shocked even me. No wonder I was not given correct treatment. Amongst the many defamatory statements my kidney disease, bacterial cystitis, eventual Medullary Sponge Kidney and undiagnosed IC were at times diagnosed as the following:

- Hysteria
- Long term personality disorder, and is convinced she has some major urinary disease, (from a GP I saw only ONCE in 1975.)
- Clinging to the belief she has a physical disorder
- Has a woeful inadequate personality
- Needs psychiatric treatment for her 'imaginary' disease (many times) Refuses to accept that her disease is psychological (many times)
- Long standing problems of mental health (unspecified) and untrue Dr C of the Kent homeopathic had written that at no time did this patient appear 'morbid or psychotically depressed' (well that's good news isn't it!)

With a pack of lies like that on my notes was it any wonder that I did not receive proper treatment. Also uncovered was the TRUTH. I was given antibiotics continually for nineteen years because infection HAD been found MANY times and I had been lied to. There SHOULD have been a diagnosis of IC at the latest by 25th April 1978. (TWENTY-TWO YEARS before it was actually diagnosed. IC was suspected in April 1978 and the diagnosis 'lost'. A letter from a psychiatrist at Wembley in November 1974 confirmed that my urinary symptoms were REAL. This was ignored.

Scarring of the bladder wall was found as early as 1977 – suggesting IC. And this diagnosis was suggested and 'lost'. A biopsy report was 'lost'.

In May 1978 a consultant effectively diagnosed IC, though not by name.

And hydro dilation (stretching of the bladder) of which I had a few treatments actually was the treatment then for IC. So in theory I was being treated for IC even though its existence was denied.

It was also confirmed that even THEN hydro dilation was a useless and outdated treatment (it's still being used today!)

In August 1980 at the homeopathic classic petechial haemorrhage spots had been discovered in the bladder wall – a classic sign of IC.

My bladder SHOULD have been removed by the NHS at the LATEST April 1981.

Well so much for 'imagination'.

When my solicitor, consultant urological surgeon, and a barrister met in London, it took three hours get to the truth, prove gross negligence, and prove my disease was not and never had been mental/psychological.

Then I spent the last hour with the barrister explaining that now one of the main consultants involved in the negligence was dead. All the others would shovel it on him and you could not sue the dead (what a pity!). How the NHS would LIE their way out of it. (They are good at that.)

If I won the case the pay out would not be very high

as it did not kill me. Apparently if I was dead it would be much higher – but not much use!

It would cost much more to actually bring the case than I would receive in compensation. If I lost I would lose everything, and would spend the rest of my life paying off the debt.

On the way home M said to me, "You have taken it very well."

That was 21st May 2002 – tomorrow is my birthday – well happy birthday. No I did not take it well. I went into delayed shock. I had to leave the Alexandra, one of the reasons being I could not work in an atmosphere where there were consultants.

I still to this day want justice (not money, JUSTICE).

One of the good things to come out of it though was officially proving I was not and never had been mentally ill, that my disease was physical.

Apart from two severe kidney infections I have not had much further kidney illness. I am supposed to go back regularly for kidney scans to check that my kidneys are coping. I don't bother. For someone who was not supposed to see 25 and I am now 61, I think I will be OK. Besides I would not trust the NHS to scan a bloody hamster. And I have told them so – I hope that is written on the notes too.

Since then I have made two visits to the Sussex County Hospital. The first one was for a blood test. I would describe the atmosphere as a cattle market – but cattle are not allowed to be treated like that – there is a law against it.

The second was when I developed an infection around the stoma. I had never met my stoma nurse but had spoken to her on the phone and heard she had a good reputation.

I agreed to go to the Sussex County instead of

requesting a home visit. Where I saw her deputy. Now I admit the after care in London could not be faulted – first class – so I supposed that as my operation was done due to NHS negligence I may be treated with a little courtesy. Not a chance.

"I know what I am doing," young bitch snapped at me. "I have been doing this job for years."

She must have started when she was an embryo!

Bitch insisted I change the flanges I wore to a different type.

"No, I prefer these."

"I am the doctor, you will do as I say. I will change your prescription."

She insisted I change the flange then to the type she wanted me to wear. And gave me two more. The first failed before I left the hospital – 1 hour.

The second lasted 2 hours, the third did not last the night. I made sure my prescription was not changed and never went back to the Sussex County.

Sadly, I have found from ladies I helped that this attitude is not unusual.

I saw a GP in 2008. First I saw the practice nurse who confirmed I had a severe infection which was dangerous and I MUST see the GP to have antibiotics. So I went in and explained that the nurse had sent me in and why so what did he say to me?

"What are these scars on your arms?"

I did not see a doctor again until November 2014 (then it was for a cracked rib and the pain was unbearable). While in the busy local chemist the pharmacist informed the shop in a loud voice, "We don't usually dispense these, they are controlled drugs!" The controlled drug was morphine – the one I should have been on years ago if someone had bothered to admit the pain existed – you could not make it up.

I also believed that my experiences were unique. No-one else could have gone through what I had gone through. No-one else could have been told for so long that their disease was 'psychological'.

I was soon to learn that not only was I NOT unique but my experience was not that uncommon either, and worse now in 2014 so many years after finding out the truth there are STILL consultants who are telling women their IC/bacterial cystitis is 'psychological'. Worse there are women who actually believe them! How do I know – well of course it did not finish there in 2002. I wanted to use my experiences to help other women, to guide them through the maze, and over the next ten years I was to learn a lot about the way women are treated by the NHS and a lot about human nature.

Having qualified in Iridology in 1994 and to practice Nutrition in 1999, and having got to the truth, which needed to be done, before I could move on. I felt confident I could put all my knowledge, both professional and personal experience to use and help women in my position.

Anyway back to 2002.

In May 2002, a few days after the consultation in London, I went on holiday to Italy. Sounds boring doesn't it? Everyone goes on holiday, well I had not had a holiday in twenty years, with one exception when I had gone to Spain with friends and of course it was ruined by IC. So to have a holiday and be free of pain and illness was to me a miracle.

Meanwhile at work I was still in shock over what I had

discovered, and the facts now openly admitted that the NHS had wrecked my life.

In late 2002 I contacted B again, met her and asked her if she ever heard from P. Yes, they were still in contact and she gave me her address, like a fool I wrote to her. Why? I still ask myself that. Sometimes the past is best left alone, we had a normal phone conversation, and for a while we kept in touch. Meanwhile I continued to go to the meetings for the Alternative health group at the Alex.

My final meeting was in June 2003, a female consultant stated that it was up to the consultant whether a child had complementary alternative treatment.

"Should not the parents also have a say in the matter, considering it was THEIR child?" I asked.

She glared at me and said, "All consultants make mistakes."

Obviously my views on the NHS had been broadcast, I had never seen her, spoken to her before, so why make this comment? What a pity no-one had told me this when I first became ill!

So I carried on with domestic work – at least it was regular and paid. When I did see clients at home it was always for Bach, as everyone was now obsessed with 'stress'.

In April 2004 I had a phone call from P. Obviously B had been discussing me with her and told her about my cystectomy.

"You need help, why don't you have therapy?" she told me.

Great, a woman who has not seen me for twenty-four years decides I am mental because she hears I have had a diseased bladder removed – you couldn't make it up. Still it made a change from 'you are in some self created hell.'

In a further phone call (a year later) she told me she was training to be a counsellor and why didn't I have counselling? I refrained (with great difficulty) from telling her what I thought of that idea and why! I have not contacted her since.

Chapter 16

Moving On

In 2007 via COBF, I ran my own small group and carried on with correspondence and phone contacts. I heard from ladies who were being made worse by their treatments but were too afraid to tell their consultants in case they 'upset them' and were refused treatment. Ladies who were told their disease was all due to 'stress', ladies whose doctors had given up on them and told they were incurable and to live with it (especially if they were elderly).

Well I had lots of plans, including helping ladies with Nutrition, using Iridology to try to find out what was causing their IC, Bach Flower remedies to help with the emotional side etc. Also home visits to ladies who were too ill to come, and helping them walk through the maze of NHS.

I went into it with my eyes open. I knew there was no Alternative/ Complementary painkiller, no alternative to surgery, etc BUT it was now being recognised that there WAS a place for Alternative/Complementary medicine in the treatment of IC. It was now recognised there was a DIET connection. Things were moving on. At last. I had something to offer. So in 2007 the group began, and although it was a very small group, it was for a while successful, although no-one was very interested in alt./comp side a little was shown, and it helped especially in relation to allergy, two ladies had cystectomies. I learned of a private clinic in London which had a good reputation, I learned of good consultants in London, and the local ones who were good, and who to avoid. The group ran for four years.

Over the last ten years things have changed so much, there are now so many treatments mentioned in COB, also interesting articles in the press. Alternative/Complementary treatments have finally broken through the barrier, and are becoming known. It is accepted that diet is 95% effective in the treatment of IC, the allergy connection is recognised, research is being done worldwide, it is finally admitted that IC is NOT a psychosomatic/psychological disease but 100% PHYSICAL. Although I still meet many ladies who are convinced that their IC is caused by 'stress'!

In November 2011 it was officially recognised (in print) that IC is a severe disability (and about time), BUT – the mercury connection is still to be recognised and accepted.

Chapter 17

Lifting the Stone

On 14th August 2012 I went back to UCL. (39 years since I was there last.) So what has changed? For a start it was now supposed to be a 'flagship hospital' to be fair, ladies in my group have told me this. There is a research centre, a professor of medicine who in his own words abhors the groundless speculative theories about psychological causes and states. "Our cardinal lesson has been to LISTEN very carefully to what our patients describe."

Excellent – what a pity he did not work there 39 years ago! And states the following:

- Fresh microscopy misses   35% of infections
- Routine culture misses   50%
- Dipstick test misses   60-70%
- We do not use urethral or bladder distention. We have found evidence of MUCH untreated infection. Our bio microbial studies showed much infection hiding in the cells these cause low grade infection. Occasionally these colonies grow and burst from the cells causing symptoms of acute infection. Hidden inside these cells bacteria escape antibiotic and immune attack. So there you have it. Hidden infection, NOT psychological/ psychosomatic/stress etc simple biology, simple common sense. Missed for thirty-nine years.

How many lives have been ruined, how many unnecessary years of illness and pain. How many women carry on their medical notes the slur that their disease is psychological?

As I left the hospital I stopped at the 'work of art' outside the main entrance. I had to, I had read about this artwork in the papers and the cost of it, and I just had to see it for myself, because even I with all my experience of this country's health service found it hard to believe this one.

There at the entrance is a large glossy pebble. People in this country are dying on trolleys. Elderly people are left lying in their own excrement and urine as there is a chronic staff shortage. People are dying of cancer on waiting lists. Doctors are making mistakes because they do not speak or understand English. And at the same hospital where the wrecking of my life began, the lies that were to ensure I would never obtain the correct treatment, be taken seriously, or because of one man's incompetence I was wrongly labelled a 'head case' until 2002 when I proved this was a lie, a ridiculous sum of money is spent on a stone for dogs to piss on.

Still things have changed in some ways. Then it was not possible for patients to see what was written on their notes. Anything could and was written. I am NOT alone I am among many many thousands of women who have been wrongly labelled 'head cases', because some consultant does not know what is wrong and instead of admitting it tells a woman her disease is 'psychological' or 'stress' which is the current trendy word.

One thing has NOT changed. Many women do sincerely believe that their IC/cystitis etc IS caused by stress because a doctor says so. Stress is trendy, women who have contacted me and declare, "Mine is all caused by stress," or "my IC was caused by a stressful event."

"Now you no longer have the 'stressful event' why do you still have it?" Blank look/silence – never considered that one!

The data protection act of 1994 allowed patients to look at their medical notes. How many bothered? How many questioned? Admittedly it was not easy then, I tried it. Yes there was a get out clause. The notes will not be revealed if the doctor considers it is not in the patient's interest. Or in my case not in the doctor's interest.

All along I strongly suspected that my notes carried lies/slurs and defamatory statements. This was denied. I proved that my GP had written to a hospital telling a pack of lies but could do nothing about it, as I was not supposed to see the letter. But I KNEW. I knew this slur had followed me from hospital to hospital, even if I could not then prove it.

When the central computer idea was thought of I opted out immediately. I knew I would only be allowed to see what the NHS wanted me to see. That notes could be hidden/destroyed/seen by any Tom, Dick or Harriet who knew how to hack into a computer. So now the system has failed – people are slowly catching on. Pity it wasted so much money though!

So the first thing any woman needs to do is to 'lift the stone' see what is crawling underneath. So where to from here?

Your GP consultant does not know how to treat you, you have been labelled 'incurable' told to go off and live with it. Maybe offered some useless psychobabble mumbo jumbo. What now? You begin your OWN search.

Shall we start with the blindingly obvious. The kidneys. From the age of thirteen when it was discovered that there was obviously something wrong with my kidneys, and my GP did not know what and as far as I know did not even test for infection! Until I began to have the first symptoms of cystitis it was obvious to ME that there must be a connection. Unfortunately it was not so obvious to the NHS who in the twenty-nine years I was ill with infections and including often kidney infections did not have the basic common sense to connect the two! Hello – kidneys and bladder are connected! And I don't mean just by the ureters!

Kidneys and bladder are made from the same tissue, they are an organ system, they are both parts of an excretory process. What affects, irritates inflames one will obviously affect/inflame/irritate the other – common logic!

Kidneys filter the blood. What is in the blood that should not be, that can irritate, inflame the kidneys and bladder? Kidneys are part of the whole body as is the bladder. They are not different parts. Separate. What is happening in the rest of the body? What other symptoms/diseases do you or members of your family have. Has your GP ever asked?

Systemic Lupus Erythmatous is seen in 5% of IC patients. In 75% of patients with the disease the kidneys/bladder are also affected. It affects women/men on a ratio of 9.1 (as does IC). 5% may not sound a lot but 5% in epidemiology is an epidemic.

Ever been asked if there is diabetes in the family/been tested for it? I was ten years into my cystitis/IC before anyone had the sense to test me for it.

"Why have you not been tested before?" asked the GP (female).

"The NHS," I replied.

The mercury connection. I was once described by one person as, "That bloody woman who blames mercury fillings for every disease." This man had a mouth full of fillings (probably still does!) and a list of symptoms/

diseases as long as your arm. But mercury is safe, his dentist said so! I do NOT blame mercury for every disease/symptom etc but I DO ask all my clients if they have mercury fillings and if so advise them to consider having a test for metal poisoning. Some get as far as their doctor/dentist who says I am talking rubbish – so that's it.

I know of IC patients who have had their fillings removed and chelating treatment and have at the time of contact a major improvement in their symptoms. The others I do not know what happened they never got back to me.

So a brief history of mercury. The word 'quack' comes from quaksilber or quicksilver an old fashioned name for mercury.

Over 2000 years ago Pliny the Elder wrote – Mercury is a poison and has no business being in medicine. Mercury was KNOWN to be poisonous by the medical dentists in 1830 and banned from practice in 1843 (USA.)

In 1984 the American Dental Association stated that when mercury is combined with the metals used in dental amalgam its toxic properties are made harmless.

What was NOT published in 1984 by the ADA was the following.

"All amalgam scraps should be salvaged and stored in a tightly closed container, covered by sulphide solution, contaminated disposable materials should be placed in plastic bags and sealed before disposal. Health and environmental agencies should be consulted for methods of disposing of the contaminated items, (and all that BEFORE 'health and safety' was thought of.)

In other words mercury scrap is not safe in the rubbish bin but it is safe in your mouth! It's also CHEAP which is why NHS dentists use it! The next thing I am told is, "I don't have any mercury fillings so that cannot be the cause of my IC."

"Had any in the past?"

"Oh yes I had them drilled out and replaced with white – they look better." "Were you still breathing while this process was going on?"

"Of course, bloody silly question."

"So you were breathing in the vapour from the fillings which is much more dangerous than the solid metal."

"My dentist does not think so."

"Does your dentist know that dentists using mercury for fillings are four times as likely to die from a brain tumour than your average man in the street?"

"I told him what you said, he said he could not remember telling me that or reading anything in dental literature to that effect."

Oh dear – when mercury vapour hits the brain memory is the first to go.

So now we look at the diseases/symptoms signs caused by mercury poisoning from amalgam fillings.

These are NOT anecdotal but actual recordings in medical literature.

• Chronic kidney disease
• Nephritic syndrome
• Bacterial cystitis
• Interstitial cystitis
• Frequent/urgent/painful urination
• Systemic Lupus Erythematous   5% of IC patients
• IBS/colitisnearly   100% of IC patients to some degree
• Chronic fatigue syndrome   10% of IC patients
• Thyroid disease .... common in IC patients

Classic symptoms of mercury poisoning:

- Frothy bubbles in the urine
- Metallic taste in the mouth (can be due to other things)
- Mouth ulcers (not due to 'stress' as is a common belief.

In a study of 1320 patients with mercury fillings 64% reported frequent urination.

Why does mercury cause IC?

The body sees mercury for what it is – a poison.

It does what it is programmed to do – gets rid of it via the kidneys.

As the mercury is excreted it inflames the kidneys/ bladder – why because inflammation is the body's RESPONSE to a toxin.

Inflammation is the body's way of healing.

To explain take the common cold.

Dry sore throat, sneezing, runny nose, high temperature is not caused by the virus but by the body's response to it. Sneezing and runny nose expel the virus from the body, high temperature literally boils the virus to death.

When we start to look at symptoms as healing reactions, rather than something to be suppressed everything makes sense.

Unfortunately chronic exposure to mercury in the urine overwhelms the body's response and EVENTUALLY the continual irritation will cause chronic IC.

"I have never had a filling in my life so it can't be mercury."

I had heard it so often.

"Had any vaccines?"

"Yes, diptheria/BCG/combined diptheria, tetanus, pertussis, flu, etc." Some used to contain a Thimersol a derivative of mercury was used in these vaccines. Now phased out despite the denial it was dangerous (so why phase it out). So we look at diet. I eat a healthy balanced diet (how often I have heard that one). Lots of fish, that's healthy isn't it? Fish, especially tuna contains methyl mercury, including seafood. The sea is the most polluted place on the plant.

Grains – especially wheat are treated with methyl mercury fungicides. Also skin creams/hair dyes, cosmetics, some medications, wood preservatives (wood floors), latex and oil based paints. Cleaning materials. If you work in a hairdressers, do laboratory work, or nursing you are probably picking up mercury in some form.

Energy saving light bulbs – contain mercury, break one and you are in trouble. Mercury vapour escapes. Try to dispose of lighting tubes – difficult dustmen refuse to take them because of the danger.

On a more depressing subject a study was done in North America on the emission of mercury vapour from crematoria it was estimated that by the year 2010 47.888 pounds of mercury will have been released into the environment. The vapour in the air is blown by the wind and falls as mercury rain. The rain ends up in the water pollutes the fish etc. MOST mercury in the body though comes from leaking fillings.

Why is it still being used? It's CHEAP. Why has it not been banned? Because if the truth was admitted the British Dental Association would be buried under a mountain of lawsuits.

Because the UK as usual lags behind other countries who have already banned it. Why despite the growing evidence do people still allow dentists to put it in their mouths (despite it is one of the most toxic poisons known to man.)

Because the dental/medical profession says it is safe. (So was Thalidomide!) Because people choose to believe them. Because people would rather have something cheap. Any GP can order a blood test for mercury and other heavy metals free on the NHS. They can also be done comparatively cheaply in London and other laboratories across the country.

There are "mercury free" dentists who will test. So what is the problem?

"My doctor/dentist says you are talking rubbish."

"I don't want to upset my doctor/dentist."

"I have looked on the internet – it costs thousands." At time of writing 2012 cost of filling removal between £95-£125 per filling depending on size. Cost of private mercury test about £48.

Warning

It is dangerous just to have the fillings drilled out the removal MUST be done by a practicing mercury free dentist.

So what to do now.

1. Do not listen to ANYONE who tells you your symptoms are due to stress/depression/psychological. This is a PHYSICAL disease

2. Find a good consultant. I.e. one who listens to YOU. Do not put up with rudeness, ignorance, remember you are the patient he is the service provider. You would not accept shoddy service in a supermarket – why accept it from the NHS?

3. Do your OWN research, go your OWN way, you do not need any doctor's consultants permission to have ANY treatment, be it orthodox, complementary or alternative.

4. Get tested for allergies (food and chemical), for heavy metal poisoning.

5. Consider your whole body, not just the part that hurts.
6. Look at the logical – kidneys and bladder are connected and are also excretory organs, what is the body getting rid of and why?
7. Are you on any medication? Diseases of the medical profession are VERY common. Many medications affect the urinary system.
8. You are ILL IC is a DISABLING illness, do not listen to anyone who says to you, "Is that all that is wrong with you? I know someone who has cancer etc."
9. Consider Complementary/Alternative treatment to work alongside orthodox you need only your OWN permission.
10 Lift the stone and see what is crawling underneath.

See your medical notes, make sure they are CORRECT. If there is any reference to your disease being labelled 'stress', 'psychological' or 'psychosomatic' get these notes altered. Via a solicitor if necessary.

Do not give up, 'incurable' is a doctor's way of saying 'I haven't a clue how to cure you.'

If all else fails contact this bloody woman. It is by being bloody minded, not listening to doctors, not believing the psychobabble bullshit that my disease was 'all in the mind' that I survived, that I am well, that I discovered the truth.

It took twenty-nine years of my life. Things ARE improving.

There are treatments now that were not available to me and many more coming to light. SOME doctors are at last taking kidney disease and the fact that it ruins lives seriously. One day it will be seen as important as cancer, heart disease, Alzheimer's. One day there will be a cure. I hope I live to see it. Clients are telling me they know of the mercury connection. Clients are listening and going to the dentist I recommended. Clients are getting well.

I have come through the maze.

I look back on the hell I have been through, and I still ask why.

Chapter 18

The Allergy Connection

When I first started suspecting allergy as a possible cause no-one had ever heard of it. Enviromental medicine, allergists etc were all quacks.

Gradually over a period of at least ten years the truth began to filter through. First food colouring affecting children causing hyperactivity, then the gluten/wheat connection causing some cases of IBS. Food allergy/ intolerance DID cause disease.

COB admitted the connection and printed a list of foods that may cause or aggravate IC.

Unfortunately this was a general list, now it has been learned that what affects one person does not affect another, it is not possible to give everyone the same list!

When I first went to the Burgh Heath Clinic the test that gave me immediate symptoms of kidney infection was rice, one of the more unusual allergens.

Allergy and infection go together, if you have an infection suspect also allergy, if you have allergy food intolerance suspect infection also.

The most common food to cause reaction in the bladder/kidneys is milk. When allergy hits the bladder the transitional epithelium (the cells that cause the bladder to expand) become full of allergic fluid and therefore there cannot be any expansion – milk is the main culprit.

Also gluten/wheat the second most common allergen? Could the reaction also be due to mercury picked up from the grain silos?

Potato is another one that is overlooked as it is a bland food yet it is one of the four most common allergens.

To test if you are allergic to foods, cut out the offending food for five to seven days. Do NOT do this if you suffer from asthma or epilepsy as it can be dangerous.

Test in order:

- Milk (including soya milk)
- Wheat/gluten
- Potato
- Coffee
- Tea
- Water use bottled water for drinking and cooking. Omit for ten days.

How often I have been told by doctors to drink lots of water.

Firstly drinking water will NOT help IC, you cannot 'wash out' IC, you will just make the symptoms worse.

Also chlorine is a KNOWN kidney bladder irritant it is also a poisonous gas (only the British would use it to purify drinking water!) Was IC so well known BEFORE chlorine was pumped into the water? When I inform ladies of the dangers of tap water the response is often 'yes but bottled water often has bacteria in it.'

Yes, so does the body, lots of bacteria and the body is designed to deal with bacteria but not with chlorine!

Consider first then with any diet change – cut out the chlorine.

For going you own route rather than allergy testing as follows.

Ten days with no tap water, including drinking and cooking.

1 week without milk (including cheese, butter, margarine etc)

Week 2 no wheat/gluten (see list)

Week 3 no potato or potato products also no tomatoes (same family)

Week 4 no sugar or any product with sugar

Keep a food diary does anything aggravate/cause flare ups?

Medication

Query medication. Did your symptoms begin after taking any medication including OTC medication? One medication SURGAM actually CAUSES IC.

MANY well known prescription drugs affect the kidneys and bladder. Be aware that what affects one does not affect another – it is what affects YOU that is important.

Chapter 19

Horse and Cart

'Stress'

Beware of the stress myth. Stress does not cause IC, if it did there would be an epidemic! There isn't, it doesn't.

No amount of counselling/psychiatry/psychotherapy/meditation/'opening up to the universe' visualisation/thinking positive thoughts/pretending you are a tree/(or hugging one) will make an atom of difference, and IC is NOT caused by depression either, IC MAKES you depressed.

I once had a letter from a lady who told me "I have 'resolved' my

… my - … my … Why can I not resolve my IC?"

I wrote back to her and pointed out that as IC was a PHYSICAL disease it could not be 'resolved', it needed physical treatment, she wrote back and thanked me and admitted that she had never considered that! Don't put the cart before the horse!

The Gynecological connection

I fought for 8 years to have a prolapsed womb repaired. I fought for eighteen years for a hysterectomy. I suffered continual gynecological discharge and infections due to antibiotics affecting the bacteria and at one point signs that I now know were mercury discharging from my womb where my body had dumped it. Again proving that it would have been impossible to have children.

No one connected this with kidney disease, cystitis or IC.WHY? These symptoms could not be put down to 'imagination' no gynecologist ever said I 'imagined' anything so why were they not connected?

Simply no part of the body affects the other.

Urologist could not be expected to know that my womb/discharge/gynecological infection could be a cause or connected to my IC because he was not a gynecologist and a gynecologist could not be expected to connect cystitis/IC/etc with gyneo symptoms because he was not a urologist. This rubbish was written in a medical report to my solicitor.

Funny I worked out the connection very early.

Hello real world calling womb/vagina/ovaries can cause problems in the bladder area. It's not rocket science.

I received a letter from a lady early on in my work who was having the usual problems with the NHS not taking her seriously. As well as the usual symptoms, she told me she feared that she had cancer. In the first letter X described typical signs of cystitis. I reassured her that the pain she felt although so intense was typical of IC and that it was unlikely she had cancer but to check with a urologist.

X wrote back telling me she had seen a urologist and he had confirmed she did not have cancer.

I then received a letter describing gynecological symptoms which could have been connected with IC, and again X said she feared she had cancer. I advised her to consult a gynecologist and she wrote back again and said he had confirmed she did not have cancer.

Correspondence continued for over a year. X still saying

she was afraid she had cancer as the pain of the IC was so intense. Me reassuring her that as she had seen both a gynecologist and a urologist and both had confirmed she did not have cancer, then it was highly unlikely BOTH could have been wrong and that intense pain was normal in IC. But if she was still worried to get another opinion. (I thought X was a lady who had an abnormal fear of cancer).

I did not hear from X for a couple of months then I received a letter giving other symptoms that did not make sense, they were not normal IC symptoms so I advised her of this and to see another specialist. Again a gap of some weeks and then a phone call from X's husband. "X has gone into hospital." I was about to say how glad I was that something was being done for this poor woman when Z said, "They have found X has end stage ovarian cancer."

How could two specialists have missed it? X died.

Now when ladies contact me worried that IC may be cancer but they have been told that it is not and they are still worried I advise them to get a third opinion and a fourth, fifth and sixth if you are still worried. The medical profession have finally admitted that the pain in end stage IC as bad as the pain in end stage cancer.

Mercury in Retrograde

The weird and wacky side of Complementary/Alternative therapy. It would be assumed that as I tried alternative/complementary therapy for twenty years, studied it, then qualified as one even though it did not cure me it kept me sane and gave me hope so I would always recommend it, WRONG. Idiots.

Among the ones I have personally met: three homeopaths:

1   told me my IC was because I was in some self inflicted personal hell

2   decided as that due mostly to the IC I did not have sex I must be a lesbian, (I am not) and that was what was causing my disease.

3   One told me that it was all due to the attempted murder by my mother. Luckily I did not believe them as all three were wrong. Not surprisingly I would not recommend homeopathy.

A (male) healer tried to tell me sex would cure me. It gets weirder – there is a theory that UTI is caused by ritualistic satanic abuse – (often dug up by counsellors in the Recovered memory syndrome) which now thankfully has been exposed, chances are if you do not remember it, it did not happen. Genuine abuse has a memory.

IC is not caused by some deep dark secret hidden in the subconscious. How easy it would have been for me to blame my kidney disease/bacterial cystitis and then IC on child abuse, after all my mother trying to murder me happened a few months before the first symptoms. How easy to go along the 'psychological' route, and blame this instead of the mercury fillings that were put in at around the same time.

Along with the above the therapies that will NOT help/cure IC.

- Angels
- Fairies
- Resolving
- Positive thinking
- Visualisation

Alternative/Complementary therapies that DO help IC and UTI.

- Chinese herbal – good success rate with bacterial cystitis/IC Acupuncture – as above but MAY take ten to twelve treatments before success is noted.
- Diet/allergy
- Healing
- Reflexology – to balance the body in general rather than directly treat IC.
- Iridology – which in some cases can immediately find the cause that has been missed.

Iridology connection

It was not until I trained to be an Iridologist and discovered for myself that 50% of my kidney disease/IC was caused by mercury poisoning and 100% of my oromandibular dystonia.

Had I not trained I would probably to this day still be looking for the cause of my IC. So how did I find out, and how does it work?

First Iridology is NOT a trendy new treatment it was mentioned in the bible. Briefly as in reflexology where the sole of the foot is a map of the body so the iris (coloured part of the eye) is also.

The stroma of the iris (body of connective tissue) contains approximately 28,000 blind nerve endings. These nerves can be traced back to an area within the thalamus of the brain known as the lateral genicular body, is it possible that here there are connections to all organs and systems throughout the body. Medical science has not yet offered an explanation for this theory. (So in theory, because there is no scientific evidence then in the words of the orthodox medical profession it cannot exist!)

There are four layers of vascular fibres in the body of the iris, and these can be seen clearly when there is an interruption of the density of the fibre structure. To make it simpler: the tower of a computer represents the body and the screen the iris. One of the advantages of Iridology is that it shows the body as a whole. More than one organ may be involved. By looking in the iris it can be seen whether your IC symptoms involve just the bladder, or other organs or parts of the body.

In my right iris 10 o'clock position, it clearly shows a bright orange spot which shows that there is a problem at the lower jaw area. Orange pigment means either blood sugar problem, diabetes or in the case of a defined spot, heavy metal deposits.

Also in the right iris at 4.45 o'clock there is a tiny black mark the size of a pin prick. This is in the bladder area and shows that the hole is deep. Black means dead tissue or end stage.

Also directly opposite the bladder area if you draw a line straight across known as the reflex arc note the medulla area of the brain. The central controller. The kick back from the pain and discomfort of IC is hitting the control centre which explains why anyone with IC pain/discomfort/infection of cystitis feels so bloody awful – it is a PHYSICAL link, not psychological or psycho anything.

So we come to the question is your IC caused by your bladder or is your bladder the target organ? See an Iridologist – get the iris checked. If the problem IS the bladder it will show up, if the problem is any other organ part of the body it will be seen clearly. If the cause is kidneys/immune/hormone/digestive/spinal/ infection/over acid body, etc. Quick, easy and non invasive.

Missing links

So now we look at the links with IC. Usually ignored by the NHS.

- Almost 100% of IC patients have IBS in some form WHY?
- 50% have allergies WHY?
- 40% familiar connection with Rheumatoid arthritis (an auto immune disease) WHY?
- Arthritis general WHY?
- Migraine 20%
- ME 10%
- Fibromyalgia 10%
- Lupus 5%
- Hypothyroidism common

Bearing in mind that if 5% of the population had flu or another infectious disease at one point it would be considered as an epidemic.

So let's look at each one in turn.

IBS the highest only an idiot would say there is no connection it must be a coincidence!

The Chinese have a saying 'disease enters via the mouth.' What is in the mouth? Usually food! So first question is, is it caused or aggravated by something I am eating/drinking?

Second question do I have mercury fillings, root canals etc which will release mercury or nickel. Mercury leaves the body via the digestive tract.

What medication am I taking? Is my IBS due to infection e.g. undiagnosed E. Coli which can get into the bloodstream and round to the kidneys?

If the colon is not working 100% waste that cannot leave the body in this way will be dumped onto the kidneys. The digestive and urinary tract were originally formed from the same tissue what affects one will affect the other.

So we move onto allergy 50% allergy causes inflammation. Inflammation and allergy go together. Has your doctor suggested that you try an elimination diet beginning with milk and dairy (the number 1 for IBS and kidney problems?) Followed by wheat/gluten along with milk the number one for IBS? Has he/she suggested allergy tests, if not, why not? Rheumatoid arthritis/lupus/fibromyalgia auto immune diseases ever been tested.

Migraine is commonly an allergic or low blood sugar reaction. Have your thyroid levels checked – a high percentage of IC patients have thyroid problems.

Are you drinking fluorinated water along with chlorine this may be the cause. Both affect the digestive and urinary tract. The thyroid gland needs iodine to produce thyroxin fluoride displaces iodine.

Calcium levels diminish as fluoride levels rise – and GI tract can be damaged. Dangerously high fluoride levels accumulate in many organs including the kidneys and bladder.

There are comparative similarities between key factors of ME and those seen in the early stages of fluoride poisoning. Fluoride added to water is hydroflurosilic acid or silicofluoride a waste product of fertilizer. Fluoride forms a strong bond with amides which are formed when amino acids join to form a protein. This can cause chromosonal damage, and if the protein is distorted the immune system will not recognize it. Which is turn will trigger allergic gastrointestinal reactions.

<u>At least it is not cancer (and other useless comments.)</u>

At least it is not cancer/be thankful you have not got cancer/you are not going to die are you – so that is OK isn't it? NO IT BLOODY WELL ISN'T!

And the other useless 'help' that has been given to me and other IC sufferers by those who have not had the disease.

1   Perhaps it will clear up when you get married/have a baby, (female relative)
2   Why don't you get a boyfriend, then it will go away. (Female relative)
3   Why don't you have sex (male doctor)
4   Why don't you get out more, say go for a coach trip (female work colleague)
5   I wish I had your disease then I would be nice and slim like you (female work colleague)
6   Why don't you mix with people then it will go away (female relative)
7   You look well dear (when I had just said I felt like death warmed up) (female relative)
8   You are in some sort of self inflicted hell (weird homeopath)
9   I know someone who had that, they died of kidney failure in the end/committed suicide.
10 Why don't you see a psychiatrist/counsellor/meditate/ etc numerous times male and female.

Should you wish to remain a friend with someone who has IC the above should be avoided.

It is now 2014 the truth about mercury poisoning cannot be hidden anymore – the lid is about to blow.

It has finally been established that IC is a purely physical disease – now that IS a breakthrough.

Remission

What is not well known but it happens more often than is generally publicised, is that IC may go into remission. This can last anything from a few months to twenty years.

There is also a theory that IC is caused by a virus that burns itself out after few years. There IS hope. One day there WILL be a cure.

Poem Rays Of Hope (adapted from an original poem)

I said the sun will shine my beams
Of love and hope on those who dream
Of a life away from pain and ill
Who through their suffering fight on still

Who never give up
Who never give in
Who against all odds
Believe they will win

And then one day
I met the one
And gave my thanks to the burning sun
I kept on hoping
It never died
And now I am free, the sun replied

My precious child I never left
Though clouds obscured my rays
I have been there with you from the start
And will be all your days

I gave you hope when there was none
I took away your pain
I gave you back your health and life
Go out and do the same

I hope in some small way I have done just that.

Chapter 20

Nothing new under the sun

UTI. Bladder infections, cystitis is not new. We may hear much more about it now but it has existed since time began. The ancient Egyptians knew of it, so did Pliny, so did the Greeks. They all knew of herbs that would treat it.

Obviously herbs will not have the same dramatic effect as antibiotics, they work much more slowly, and admittedly they did not work for me but I was well into the end stage of IC before I used them.

Also as many herbs work synergistically it is preferable to see a qualified herbalist. However – it was known by Pliny that the herb Couchgrass cured ulcers of the bladder and cystitis, and the plant Agrimony, cured chronic bladder disorders.

Hippocrates knew that Golden Rod, cured bladder inflammation. Sweet Corn Silk was known by the American Indians as a cure for acute cystitis.

Marshmallow was known by the ancient Greeks to cure cystitis and inflammation, also the Egyptians and Greeks knew the herb Thyme cured urinary tract infections and it is said that bacilli are known to be dead within 35/40 minutes after consuming thyme.

Common mallow was known as a cure for UTI by Pythagoras.

Of all the herbal books I have read in many the list for

treating cystitis, UTI, bladder disorders is the longest in the index.

These herbs must have WORKED or they would not have been used or recorded.

Also some of the more well known ones.

Berberis – prevents bacteria including E. coli sticking to bladder surface Uva Ursi – prevents and treats UTI especially E. coli

Cranberry juice and blueberry juice are well known in the treatment of E. coli but the juice is very high in sugar and you would need to drink 1 litre a day to achieve the effect. Cranberry is available in tablet form.

A word of caution

On 12th August 2000 I was lucky, very lucky, Miss JM gave me a cystectomy and gave me my life back. I had to beg for it, plead for it, as normally cystectomies are only done in cases of advance cancer.

IC is not going to kill you so it is not worth the risk, is the NHS attitude and of course cystectomies cost money don't they. And in my case giving me one would prove that the NHS was 100% wrong and prove I did not imagine my disease. Oh dear.

I often wondered why I had to wait 20 years in the end stage of a disease, apart from the fact that the NHS did not want me to know it existed. Now I know.

G was a member of my group. Having suffered IC and similar symptoms for most of her life, and like me suffered from the NHS who were no help and often rude and indifferent.

The only way forward so I believed was to give her details of my operation and how it had helped me. I did not exactly talk her into the treatment but I did encourage her. G found a hospital in London at last. A good hospital one who at last began to listen, take an interest and tried to do something to help, she was thrilled. Then their attitude changed to her.

Still we went ahead G was given a date for her operation, it went ahead.

I was thrilled for her. I had hoped for months she would have this done.

I told her of the new life ahead of her. Although no longer coming to the group we kept in touch. G found it hard to adjust. There were complications, finally after two years G told me she was happier, she had adjusted.

Then came the letter telling me she had to have the operation done again – something had gone wrong. The second operation did not sound as if it was any better than the first. Each Christmas and on her birthday we exchanged cards. Things did not sound much better.

Finally in 2014 I sent her a birthday card and received a phone call from her partner. G had died last year. Not from natural causes, but from the complication of the THIRD Operation to correct the mistakes of the last two. Also while consulting my specialist nurse following the operation she told me, "They have done a good job on you, I have seen many bodge ups."

CHOOSE YOUR SURGEON WITH CARE – WORD OF MOUTH IS THE BEST RECOMMENDATION.

Surgery sounds like the answer. The one thing that will take all the pain and suffering away, and often it is – DONE PROPERLY women find the same as me – it gave them their life back. So what to do about surgery, do you take the risk?

There are other operations on offer for advanced IC,

admittedly cystectomy is the only one guaranteed to stop IC as it completely removes the bladder and something that no longer exists cannot be a problem. Can it? Often in cystectomy surgery the consultant will tell the patient he will disconnect the bladder and leave it in the body. His excuse being the surgery is not so major. The fact is it is shorter and therefore the cheaper operation and what he does NOT tell the patient is that if the cause of the IC pain is the bladder itself the old bladder left in the body can still cause pain. This has been found by patients who have had this operation. Besides, who wants a disconnected rotting organ inside them?

The Koch Pouch is a newer operation which is a Catheterisable pouch inside the body – no bag and better for by anyone who is concerned about body image. The downside is that as the pouch does not always empty completely there is the risk of infection and the patient can develop IC in the new bladder pouch.

I am not suggesting Complementary/Alternative therapy is in any way better or more successful than orthodox.

There is no Alternative painkiller and no Alternative to surgery.

However when caught in the EARLY stages cystitis/IC will respond to Complementary/Alternative therapy.

Both can help in some diseases and this includes IC work together.

Will there ever be a cure? I believe so and I hope I will see it in my lifetime. Since I had my surgery fourteen years ago so much has changed.

It is now finally accepted that IC is a PHYSICAL disease. There are many treatments for pain, including implants. There are treatments for the actual bladder including installations.

Research is being done WORLDWIDE now. The hospital where I was wrongly branded a nutcase is now a flagship hospital.

Many Holistic clinics treat IC/cystitis successfully.

So much information is available on the internet. There are support groups all over the country, including small local groups. (Contact COB Foundation – address in list of helpful contacts.)

Leading the horses

Since I began my work in helping IC patients one thing keeps coming up again and again.

"It's such an isolating illness."

Yes it is a bloody cruel painful disease that destroys lives, careers, relationships hope. I know because I have BEEN there.

There are now phone contacts/E mail/local groups. Contact/meet/share. The best treatment for you may not be in your area – be prepared to travel (I know it's hell, I travelled all over this country looking for someone to help me, trying new treatments and was ready to travel abroad if necessary.)

Sorry but no-one ever got well by staying isolated.

I was working at a Holistic Fayre recently and a lady came for a taster session for Iridology. I examined her irises correctly, told her she had problems with her kidneys, bladder which she confirmed. Cystitis and kidney infections. Asked her if she had any mercury fillings,

"Yes a mouth full, all old and corroding."

I very briefly explained the dangers and how ill it had made me. Then I gave her details of dentists, etc.

"I have to PAY?" she said shocked.

"Yes, but isn't your health more important than money?"

"But I ONLY have cystitis and kidney infections."

Leading the horses to water is easy – making them drink is harder!

Silent Loom
Not till the loom is silent
And shuttles cease to fly
Does God reveal the pattern
Explain the reason WHY.

Now after all these years I can see the pattern. I can be above the maze and see where I went wrong. I was naive, I thought doctors healed, I thought doctors knew what they were doing. I thought doctors were truthful. Now it is out in the open, some doctors lie, some doctors cover up, some doctors NEVER admit they are wrong. I see the pattern but I still ask WHY – I am only human.

Helpful Contacts

The COB Foundation
Kings Court
17 School Road
Hall Green
Birmingham
B28 8JG
0121 702 0820
www.cobfoundation.org
Info@cobfoundation.org
Facebook.com/COB Foundation

The Association for Mercury Free Dentistry
The Weathervane
22a Moorend Park Road
Cheltenham
Glos
01242 226918
www.mercuryfreedentistry.org.uk

The Guild of Iridologists
Jackie Day
Coombe Head Farm
Tongue End, Okehampton
Devon
EX20 1QL

Biolab Medical Unit
The Stone House
9 Weymouth Street
London
W1W 6DB
0207 636 5959
Email: info@biolab.co.uk
www.biolab.co.uk
Tests for allergy/mercury/heavy metals

Janet Baird, author of *Through a Maze Blindfold*
bairdjanet36@gmail.com

Acknowledgements

With grateful thanks to

Miss J McDonald M.B.B.S F.R.C.S. (Ed) Dip Urol (London)
The late Antony Newbury
The late Dr. Goodman
Dr A Hibberd
Jessica
Shan
Pearl
Dr. John Mansfield
Pat
Lesley
Melanie----